Total Lawfare

This book advocates for a novel doctrine of 'total lawfare' as part of a comprehensive approach to modern hybrid warfare.

The book begins by introducing the military concept of 'limited lawfare' in the context of modern geopolitical conditions. It proceeds to set out a conceptual history of lawfare in the West, highlighting conceptual shortcomings and NATO's limited capabilities in this branch of hybrid warfare. It then provides a comparative case study and strategic threat assessment of the Chinese concept of 'unrestricted lawfare'. Against this, the book grounds an ethical doctrine of 'total lawfare' within the Western jurisprudential tradition and translates this into practice as a key pillar of modern defense strategy under the rule of law. The book concludes by advocating for a Thielian 'New Defense' industry centered upon 'total lawfare' as a legitimate and effective Western response to enemy aggression.

The book will be of interest to academics, policy-makers, and students working in the fields of lawfare, jurisprudence, and military law.

Patrick S. Nash is Founder Director of the Pharos Foundation in Oxford. He was previously a Visiting Fellow at the Faculty of Theology and Religion at Oxford, and a Research Fellow at the Woolf Institute in Cambridge. He has taught jurisprudence, public law, criminal law, tort law, and family law at the universities of Bristol and Newcastle. He was called to the Bar of England and Wales in 2019 and is a member of Lincoln's Inn. His first monograph, *British Islam and English Law*, was published by Cambridge University Press in 2022.

Deniz Guzel practices commercial litigation and arbitration at the international law firm, CMS, with experience in class action disputes and public international law. Previously, he practiced international criminal law at the Extraordinary Chambers in the Courts of Cambodia and worked at various Westminster-based think tanks. Deniz holds an MA with Distinction in International Peace and Security from King's College London and an LLB from the University of Bristol, where he won the prize for Roman Law.

Total Lawfare

New Defense and Lessons from China's Unrestricted Lawfare Program

Patrick S. Nash and Deniz Guzel

R Routledge
Taylor & Francis Group

LONDON AND NEW YORK

First published 2024
by Routledge
4 Park Square, Milton Park, Abingdon, Oxon OX14 4RN

and by Routledge
605 Third Avenue, New York, NY 10158

Routledge is an imprint of the Taylor & Francis Group, an informa business

British Library Cataloguing-in-Publication Data
A catalogue record for this book is available from the British Library

Library of Congress Cataloging-in-Publication Data
Names: Nash, Patrick (Law teacher), author. | Guzel, Deniz, author.
Title: Total lawfare : new defense and lessons from China's unrestricted lawfare program / Patrick S. Nash and Deniz Guzel.
Description: Abingdon, Oxon [UK] ; New York, NY : Routledge, 2024. | Includes bibliographical references and index.
Identifiers: LCCN 2024006677 (print) | LCCN 2024006678 (ebook) | ISBN 9781032710204 (hardback) | ISBN 9781032723990 (paperback) | ISBN 9781032724003 (ebook)
Subjects: LCSH: Lawfare--China. | Military law--China--History. | Hybrid warfare--China. | China--Military policy--History. | Military readiness--Law and legislation.
Classification: LCC KNQ3735 .N37 2024 (print) | LCC KNQ3735 (ebook) | DDC 343.51/01--dc23/eng/20240214
LC record available at https://lccn.loc.gov/2024006677
LC ebook record available at https://lccn.loc.gov/2024006678

ISBN: 978-1-032-71020-4 (hbk)
ISBN: 978-1-032-72399-0 (pbk)
ISBN: 978-1-032-72400-3 (ebk)

DOI: 10.4324/9781032724003

Typeset in Times New Roman
by Deanta Global Publishing Services, Chennai, India

For Larry Siedentop, Julian Rivers, and Richard Mullender

Contents

1 Opening Moves

1.1 General Introduction

In *The Western Way of War*, the great American classicist Victor Davis Hanson famously posited that Western primacy rests upon a unique political tradition dating back to classical Greece.[1] Simply put, the Western veneration of freedom and its ancillaries – namely individualism, innovation, initiative, and introspection – bestowed an unrivaled capacity for pragmatic dynamism and cumulative learning 'which have consistently produced superior arms and soldiers.'[2] In times of war, Hanson argues, this culture predisposes its constituent nations to seek short, sharp confrontations punctuated by direct, decisive battles in which Western arms, training, and technology reliably carry the day. This is because, on this worldview, the point of any contest – whether a political domestic dispute or an armed global struggle – is to reach an undisputed outcome as quickly as possible so that citizen participants and their governments can return to the more agreeable pursuits of family life, private enterprise, and self-governance. Anything that distracts or detracts from this – especially irregular warfare and unconventional weaponry – is typically held in 'repugnance' or at least adopted reluctantly and with loud protestations as a last resort.[3]

However, the standard Western approach has proven 'embarrassingly ineffective' in protracted modern conflicts against elusive enemies employing demoralizing guerrilla and psychological tactics.[4] Whatever qualifications

---

1 Victor Davis Hanson, *The Western Way of War: Infantry Battle in Classical Greece*, 2nd ed. (Berkeley: University of California Press, 2009).
2 Victor Davis Hanson, *Carnage and Culture: Landmark Battles in the Rise of Western Power* (New York: Anchor Books, 2002), blurb.
3 See Hanson, *The Western Way of War*, 13; Adrienne Mayor, *Greek Fire, Poison Arrows, & Scorpion Bombs: Biological & Chemical Warfare in the Ancient World: Biological and Chemical Warfare in the Ancient World* (New York: Overlook, 2003); and Peter Krentz, "Deception in Archaic and Classical Greek warfare," in Hans van Wees, ed., *War and Violence in Ancient Greece* (Swansea: Classical Press of Wales, 2009), 167–200.
4 Hanson, *Carnage and Culture*, 457–459; Hanson, *The Western Way of War*, 11.

DOI: 10.4324/9781032724003-1

might be made to Hanson's sweeping thesis, he is certainly correct to note that a peculiar cultural baggage weighs upon modern Western belligerents and presents them with an equally peculiar dilemma: how does one engage with an adversary that does not adhere to the same ideals while remaining true to those very ideals oneself?[5] Nowhere is this quandary more apposite than in the emerging arenas of geopolitical competition as the world trudges from the 'foothills' to the 'mountain passes' of a new cold war.[6]

Law is one such arena and it, as the Western cliché goes, is a blunt instrument: 'It's not a scalpel. It's a club.'[7] Little wonder, then, that the obscure concept of 'lawfare' barely features in the technologically superlative arsenals of today's Western powers. Seemingly secure behind their societies' military hardware and in their WEIRD worldview (i.e. Western, Educated, Industrialized, Rich, and Democratic),[8] many of the West's best legal and military minds still regard the very notion of weaponizing law as a shocking – even unthinkable – one.[9] Indeed, far more intellectual energy has been expended over the last two centuries on valiant attempts to use law to outlaw war itself despite limited and diminishing returns.[10] This essentially Christian outlook, which tends towards an assumption of natural justice, institutional compartmentalization, and moral individualism, forms the bedrock of the Western social and world order.[11] Throughout the modern period, while European and American power waxed the world over, these assumptions have been projected – even imposed – onto other cultures.[12] Yet however inaccurate, patronizing or dismissive such 'Orientalizing' interpretations may seem to the peoples subjected to them, they also present a danger to those doing the projecting.

As Western economic and military dominance declines in relative terms, and NATO continues to lose wars against less sophisticated but more

5 Hanson, *Carnage and Culture*, 460–461.

6 Henry Kissinger quoted by Niall Ferguson, interview, *Cold War II: Niall Ferguson on the Emerging Conflict with China*, Hoover Institution, May 1, 2023, hosted by Peter Robinson, https://www.hoover.org/research/cold-war-ii-niall-ferguson-emerging-conflict-china.

7 Neil Gaiman, "Why Defend the Freedom of Icky Speech?" *Neil Gaiman* Journal, December 1, 2008, https://journal.neilgaiman.com/2008/12/why-defend-freedom-of-icky-speech.html.

8 Joseph Henrich, *The Weirdest People in the World: How the West Became Psychologically Peculiar and Particularly Prosperous* (London: Allen Lane, 2020).

9 Orde F. Kittrie, *Lawfare: Law as a Weapon of War* (Oxford: Oxford University Press, 2016), 34–35.

10 Mark Mazower, *Governing the World: The History of an Idea* (London: Penguin, 2012); Oona A. Hathaway and Scott J. Shapiro, *The Internationalists and Their Plan to Outlaw War* (London: Penguin, 2018).

11 Tom Holland, *Dominion* (London: Little, Brown, 2019); Larry Siedentop, *Inventing the Individual* (London: Penguin, 2015); Niall Ferguson, *Civilisation: The West and the Rest* (London: Penguin, 2012); Roger Scruton, *The West and the Rest* (London: Continuum, 2002).

12 This is perhaps the ultimate point of Edward Said's book, *Orientalism* (New York: Pantheon, 1978).

determined opponents across the Middle East, moralistic hubris has become a perishable luxury that Western governments can ill-afford.[13] The 'snakes' (non-state actors like Al Qaeda and ISIS) and 'dragons' (state superpowers like Russia and China) have spent decades learning from the West's mistakes and honing their methods of hybrid warfare.[14] That they have 'weaponized everything' – from refugees and energy to culture and truth itself – to create an 'age of unpeace' is precisely because the world has become so well-connected and rules-oriented, not in spite of it.[15] America and her allies have thus far proved themselves remarkably complacent in the face of the 'serious threat' posed by such techniques which are steadily 'disabling the West's [conventional] military advantage.'[16] Given this, Western hegemony has never looked more precarious should, as Graham Allison fears, the established power of the US and the rising power of China walk into the 'Thucydides Trap' and open war.[17] It is by no means unprecedented, for example, for a Western power to write off an Asian competitor as inferior before losing disastrously to them.[18] Even if geopolitical rivalry does not break out into armed conflict, 'decline is only a matter of time' unless the West rapidly develops its own capabilities for unconventional warfare.[19] How, then, to avert the eclipse? That question looms over this book, which focuses upon the concept of 'lawfare,' the branch of unconventional warfare where the West has the most 'serious catching-up to do.'[20]

This book is an unashamed attempt to help Western powers close this gap. By 'Western' or 'the West,' the authors are referring primarily to those nations of European heritage (Europe, the Americas, Australasia) within or aligned to NATO, and more loosely to those democratic Asian nations (Israel, India, Japan, South Korea, Taiwan) with historic and ongoing strategic ties to

---

13 See Mark Urban, *The Edge: Is the Military Dominance of the West Coming to an End?* (London: Little, Brown, 2015); and Sean McFate, *Goliath: Why the West Doesn't Win Wars and What We Need to Do about It* (London: Penguin, 2019).

14 David Kilcullen, *The Dragons and the Snakes: How the Rest Learned to Fight the West* (London: Hurst, 2020).

15 See Mark Galeotti, *The Weaponization of Everything: A Field Guide to the New Way of War* (Yale University Press, 2022); Peter Pomerantsev, *This Is Not Propaganda: Adventures in the War against Reality* (London: Faber & Faber, 2020); and Mark Leonard, *The Age of Unpeace: How Connectivity Causes Conflict* (Penguin, 2022).

16 Kilcullen, *The Dragons and the Snakes*, blurb.

17 See generally Graham Allison, *Destined for War: Can America and China Escape Thucydides's Trap?* (New York: Houghton Mifflin Harcourt, 2017).

18 See Richard Connaughton, *Rising Sun and Tumbling Bear: Russia's War with Japan* (London: W&N, 2004); and Max Hastings, *Vietnam: An Epic Tragedy, 1945–1975* (London: William Collins, 2018).

19 Kilcullen, *The Dragons and the Snakes*, 6.

20 Charles J. Dunlap, Jr., "Yes, there is consensus that 'lawfare' exists … but America still needs a strategy for it," *Lawfire*, September 23, 2021, https://sites.duke.edu/lawfire/2021/09/23/yes-there-is-consensus-that-lawfare-exists-but-america-still-needs-a-strategy-for-it.

the former. Notwithstanding the ceaseless controversy surrounding the term, 'Western' is here just rough shorthand for this motley assemblage of powers with a broad shared interest in countering Chinese aggression. Both authors are WEIRD analysts from Great Britain, and as such the main focus throughout falls upon the preeminent common law systems within this grouping (i.e. the US and UK). However, to avoid reaching weird conclusions, they have sought to suspend their cultural preconceptions and jettison concepts 'that fit Western academic sensibilities' by proceeding anthropologically.[21] The point is simply to take other peoples seriously so that we can better understand an adversary by understanding how they view themselves, us, and our respective places in the world. Only then can the nature and scale of any danger be assessed accurately and countered proportionately. Admittedly, any account of any great civilization or movement by any outsider will inevitably be constrained by time, space, simplification, generalization, and imperfect knowledge. Yet running the gauntlet of charges of 'essentializing' or 'cultural racism' is well worth the risk as incisive accounts of other cultures can be done well.[22] What is more, the very effort is a prudent and humanizing endeavor because it enables one to regard even the most vicious adversary as a worthy opponent deserving of respect. Indeed, one of Henry Kissinger's greatest observations was to note that history is to a country what childhood experience is to individual character.[23] As another of its best practitioners well knew, the careful study of history is perhaps the only defense against foolish theorizing, inane prejudice, wishful thinking, dark despair, and the relentless march of government folly.[24] This, then, is the spirit of the book to follow.

As for its methodology, the authors rely heavily upon law in context, comparative jurisprudence, and applied history. Taking each in turn, the book takes its omnivorous disposition towards evidence – empirical, theoretical, qualitative, quantitative, scholarly, journalistic – from the law in context movement, which further lends itself to plain-speaking argumentation.[25] Comparative jurisprudence translates this disposition into practice and proceeds from the recognition 'that existing legal institutions cannot be

21 Matthew Engelke, *Think Like an Anthropologist* (London: Pelican, 2017), 109.
22 Classic examples include Ruth Benedict, *The Chrysanthemum and the Sword: Patterns of Japanese Culture* (New York: Mariner Books, 2005); Barbara W. Tuchman, *Notes from China* (New York: Random House, 2017), and *Stillwell and the American Experience in China 1911–1945* (New York: MacMillan, 1970).
23 See generally Henry Kissinger, *World Order: Reflections on the Character of Nations and the Course of History* (London: Allen Lane, 2014).
24 See Barbara Tuchman, *March of Folly: From Troy to Vietnam* (London: Abacus, 1990), and *Practising History: Selected Essays* (New York: Knopf, 1981); see also Robert Crowcroft, "The Case for Applied History," *History Today*, Vol. 68, No. 9, September 9, 2018, https://www.historytoday.com/archive/feature/case-applied-history.
25 Patrick S. Nash, *British Islam and English Law: A Classical Pluralist Perspective* (Cambridge: Cambridge University Press, 2022), 7–8.

understood without some knowledge of their history, and therefore ... comparative jurisprudence [cannot be regarded] as a thing standing apart from historical study and discrimination.'[26] This prescribes 'an integrated view of various juristic techniques' with a view both to tracing the origins and development of the phenomenon in question, as well as acquiring the practical knowledge necessary to formulate an effective response.[27] Key to it all is applied history, which is straightforwardly an 'attempt to illuminate current challenges and choices by analyzing historical precedents and analogues.'[28] It redresses the 'culture of mutual contempt between practitioners and historians' as well as the 'history deficit' among Western policymakers who often 'know alarmingly little not just of other countries' pasts, but also of their own.'[29] This 'big tent' approach requires one to take 'a current choice or predicament and analyze the historical record to provide perspective, stimulate imagination, find clues about what is likely to happen, suggest possible interventions, and assess probable consequences.'[30] This tripartite method suggests the course of the book's central argument: that in order to wage lawfare effectively, the West must first locate a viable concept within its own intellectual tradition while drawing illuminating comparisons with its chief competitor, the People's Republic of China (hereafter referred to in shorthand as either the PRC or China). Accordingly, we begin from the first principles.

1.2 Does Lawfare Still Need an Apologia?

The development of Western lawfare, as Major General Charles J. Dunlap Jr. observes, is being hindered from the law school upwards:

> Importantly, lawfare was not – and is not – intended to assuage the penchant of academics and policy enthusiasts to put all human activity into some designated theoretical box suitable for explication in university texts. To paraphrase Steven Coll, lawfare is not law for northeastern graduate students. Rather, the target audience is principally the doers, and the goal of lawfare's development and use is wholly down-to-earth. It was, and is, an effort to find a resonating bumper sticker to help to explain to a very unique client base – military personnel and, especially, their leaders

---

26 Frederick Pollock, "The History of Comparative Jurisprudence," *Journal of the Society of Comparative Legislation*, Vol. 5, No. 1 (1903), 74.
27 F.C. Auld, "Methods of Comparative Jurisprudence," *The University of Toronto Law Journal*, Vol. 8, No. 1 (1949) 83.
28 Graham Allison and Niall Ferguson, "Applied History Manifesto" (Cambridge, Mass.: Belfer Center for Science and International Affairs, Harvard Kennedy School; October 2016), https://www.belfercenter.org/publication/applied-history-manifesto.
29 Ibid.
30 Ibid.

– how and, equally important, why the law needs to be incorporated into their thinking and planning.[31]

Before engaging the definitional controversies over the term itself, it is worth noting just how little scholarly interest it has attracted. Lawfare, to paraphrase its chief academic popularizer, was never for the academics. As a concept, it is purportedly 'intellectually plebian' with no value beyond its communicative ability to help its military doers do war with law.[32] To allow otherwise would be to turn a proper military doctrine over to the 'liberal-minded intelligentsia' and other classroom generals 'who would never own a gun.'[33] The flow of intellectual effort is unidirectional, from firm to front, and 'we should be less concerned whether or not the terminology fits neatly into the epistemology of academic theory or, for that matter, think tank salons.'[34] The academics, for their part, seem to agree: there has been only one major conference on the subject back in 2010; only one major monograph published in 2016 which devotes itself to collating disparate examples of lawfare in action; two minor theoretical works presenting incomplete conceptual histories and confused typologies of lawfare in impenetrable academese; a few short example-heavy chapters in several more recent books on broader subjects; and 'lawfare' features nowhere in standard reference texts for modern 'law' or 'war,' nor in national curricula for law schools, nor even in professional military training programs.[35] Scholarly debate over lawfare, such as it is, has gotten no further in two decades than 'warring over semantics' and a bare consensus that some such phenomenon exists.[36] The distant ruminations of academic lawyers may seem superfluous to the requirements of modern conflict, but their virtual absence is having serious consequences. As even General Dunlap concedes, 'lawfare may indeed need an *apologia* of sorts.'[37]

---

31 Charles J. Dunlap Jr., "Does lawfare need an apologia?" *Case Western Reserve Journal of International Law*, Vol. 43. No. 1 (2010), 126.

32 Dunlap, "Does lawfare need an apologia?" 128.

33 Ibid., fn 25, quoting Steve Coll.

34 Ibid., 128

35 Kittrie, *Lawfare*, 8–9; *Cristiano Zanin, Valeska Martins, and Rafael Valim, Lawfare: Waging War through Law* (Routledge Focus, 2022); Jaume Castan Pinos and Mark Friis Hau, *Lawfare: New Trajectories in Law* (Routledge Focus, 2023); Orde F. Kittrie, "Using Law as a Weapon against Nuclear Proliferation and Terrorism: The US Government's Financial Lawfare against Iran," in Jens David Ohlin et al., eds., *Between Crime and War: Hybrid Legal Frameworks for Asymmetric Conflict* (Oxford University Press, 2022) chap. 9; Galeotti, *The Weaponization of Everything* (London: Yale University Press, 2022) 145–159; Leonard, *The Age of Unpeace*, 124–128; and Jill I. Goldenziel, "Law as a Battlefield: The U.S., China, and Global Escalation of Lawfare," *Cornell Law Review*, Vol. 106 (2020), 1166–1168.

36 Dunlap, "Does lawfare need an apologia?" 142; and Dunlap, "Yes, there is consensus that 'lawfare' exists … but America still needs a strategy for it."

37 Dunlap, "Does lawfare need an apologia?" 141.

The *apologia* it has thus far received is insufficient. This is especially true in today's 'credential society' in which, using 2021 statistics as an example, almost 19,000 law students graduated from over 100 UK law schools (a record high) while in the US over 35,000 law students graduated from almost 200 US law schools (an increase on previous years).[38] That so few are taught about lawfare or study it in-depth is perpetuating chronic ignorance across the media, policy world, and government.[39] Dunlap warns that the common tendency to 'castigate the concept' whenever terrorists or hostile regimes abuse law is not only futile – the phenomenon 'is not just here to stay, but is likely to continue to grow and proliferate' – but actively harmful to Western interests because it plays to negative stereotypes of lawyers, undermines public confidence in the rule of law, and ultimately precludes an effective response.[40] Understandably, therefore, Western lawfare apologetics have been preoccupied with establishing the urgent practical and moral case for a strategy that does not yet exist, illuminating its possible forms and uses via case studies, and highlighting its myriad potential benefits over direct kinetic confrontation. A consistent theme is the central role played by law in legitimizing or delegitimizing governments, narratives, policies, and actions both in the domestic sphere and on the world stage.[41] Nevertheless, the existing literature's uncompromising pragmatism fails to provide its own compelling internal narrative as to where this phenomenon 'fits' within the Western intellectual tradition and how its place there can be 'justified.'[42]

The institutional theorist Samo Burja observes that

> it is both difficult and time-consuming to fully understand new ideas and evaluate them on their own merits. Sometimes, it is socially risky as well. As such, people will often instead evaluate the *intellectual legitimacy* of new ideas … insofar as [they are] recognized by society as respectable and reasonable.[43]

---

38 See Randall Collins, *The Credential Society: An Historical Sociology of Education and Stratification* 2nd ed. (Columbia University Press, 2019); Aishah Hussain, "Number of law graduates hits record high" *Legal Cheek*, September 22, 2022, https://www.legalcheek.com/2022/09/number-of-law-graduates-hits-record-high; and "Number of law graduates in the United States from 2013 to 2021," *Statista*, July 6, 2022;
      https://www.statista.com/statistics/428985/number-of-law-graduates-us.
39 Dunlap, "Does lawfare need an apologia?" 123, 136.
40 Ibid., 133, 137, 141.
41 Goldenziel, "Law as a Battlefield," 4–5, 13.
42 See Ronald Dworkin, *Taking Rights Seriously* (Cambridge: Harvard University Press, 1977).
43 Samo Burja, "Intellectual Legitimacy," *Samo Burja*, December 21, 2020; https://samoburja.com/intellectual-legitimacy.

This means that the acceptance and dissemination of a new idea depend less upon its inherent truth or potential utility and more upon whether enough of the right people are motivated to find it legible and unthreatening.[44] The concept of lawfare evidently has not achieved such intellectual legitimacy given that Western politicians still cast the phenomenon in 'diabolical' conspiratorial terms and attack the term itself as 'inflammatory,' 'divisive,' and 'preposterous.'[45] In 2020, for example, during the passage of the Overseas Operations (Service Personnel and Veterans) Bill through the UK Parliament, its explicit counter-lawfare dimension was attacked by the Joint Human Rights Committee in the following terms: 'It is wholly inappropriate to use this term to refer to the application of the rule of law to determine cases where injured civilians or soldiers are seeking justice.'[46] While such uncomprehending hostility is perhaps unsurprising considering that lawyers have long been one of the largest occupational groups in common law legislatures, there is clearly much legitimizing left to do among Western elites.[47]

The lawfare apologist's task is therefore really twofold: first, to assuage the northeastern graduate (and future politician) that lawfare is compatible with life under the rule of law and thereby constitutes an intellectually stimulating subject worthy of deeper scholarly engagement than it has hitherto received; and second, to demonstrate to the down-to-earth doer that the former's robust scholarship will make his own practice more comprehensible and effective. If it is ever to win the hearts and minds of the world, the West must draw from its own traditions to build confidence in the basis, limits, and applications of its own way of lawfare. Here too there is much work to do.

1.3   A Brief Conceptual History of Lawfare

In *On Human Conduct* (1975), the English philosopher Michael Oakeshott (1901–90) described two polar opposite kinds of society. At one end lay the pure civil association, an entirely rule-articulated society in which individuals

---

44 Samo Burja, "Knowledge Production and Intellectual Legitimacy," *Samo Burja*, January 12, 2021, https://samoburja.com/knowledge-production-and-intellectual-legitimacy.

45 Dunlap, "Does lawfare need an apologia?" 136; and "Legislative Scrutiny: The Overseas Operations (Service Personnel and Veterans) Bill," *House of Commons Joint Committee on Human Rights Ninth Report of Session 2019–21*, 38–39, https://committees.parliament.uk/publications/3191/documents/39059/default/#page=41.

46 "Overseas Operations (Service Personnel And Veterans) Bill Explanatory Notes," *House of Commons*, March 18, 2020, 5, https://publications.parliament.uk/pa/bills/cbill/58-01/0117/en/20117en.pdf; and "Legislative Scrutiny: The Overseas Operations (Service Personnel and Veterans) Bill."

47 "Why Lawyers Rule American Politics," *Niskanen Center*, August 25, 2021, https://www.niskanencenter.org/why-lawyers-rule-american-politics; and John Hyde, "Legal background is ticket to seat in new parliament," May 21, 2015, https://www.lawgazette.co.uk/news/legal-background-is-ticket-to-seat-in-new-parliament/5048967.article.

and groups are free to pursue their own diverse ends and remain united only in their mutual acknowledgment of general, non-instrumental rules of conduct. At the other lay the pure enterprise association, a society dedicated to the state's organizational goal against which the legitimacy and efficacy of laws are measured and to which members are expected to dedicate their lives.[48] For him, the type of society best adapted to the opportunities and challenges of lawfare would lie in 'unstable equipoise' between the two.[49] According to Oakeshott, modern Western society most closely and consistently resembles a civil association, but, during great crises, it might temporarily acquire some moderated features of an enterprise association which it would not normally countenance.[50] As much seems to have been true at the time Colonel Charles J. Dunlap, Jr. of the United States Air Force (as he then was) coined his seminal definition of 'lawfare' as 'the use of law as a weapon of war' in the grim fall of 2001.[51]

No etymological or semiotic study has been able to trace the concept back any further than the late 1990s as a way of describing 'a new relationship between law and war.'[52] What infrequent, throwaway uses there are date from 1957 and refer to everything from the squabbling of divorcees through nasty courtroom tactics to discounted lawyers' airfares.[53] The only semi-philosophical treatment of the term came from two Australian hippies writing in 1975 who used it to denote the tendency of adversarial legal systems to escalate conflicts between parties instead of facilitating 'humane justice' through mediative 'community law' concerned with 'harmony, peace and love.'[54] Not without cause, then, could Dunlap claim to have invented a novel Western doctrine when nothing like a Vegetius *De Legibus* or a Clausewitz *Vom Rechtskriege* had ever before been written.[55]

---

48 Michael Oakeshott, *On Human Conduct* (Oxford: Oxford University Press, 1975), 199–206.

49 Richard Mullender, "Transmuting the Politico-Legal Lump: Brexit and Britain's Constitutional Order," *Cardozo Law Review*, Vol. 39, No. 1 (2018), 1024.

50 Paul Franco, *The Political Philosophy of Michael Oakeshott* (New Haven: Yale University Press, 1990), 219.

51 Charles J. Dunlap, Jr., "Law and Military Interventions: Preserving Humanitarian Values in 21st Century Conflicts," presented at *Humanitarian Challenges in Military Interventions Conference* (2001), 2.

52 Dunlap, "Yes, there is consensus that 'lawfare' exists … but America still needs a strategy for it"; and Susan W. Tiefenbrun, "Semiotic Definition of Lawfare," *Case Western Reserve Journal of International Law*, Vol. 43, No.1 (2010), 29–60.

53 Leila Nadya Sadat and Jing Geng, "On Legal Subterfuge and the So-Called 'Lawfare' Debate," *Case Western Reserve Journal of International Law*, Vol. 43, No. 1 (2010), 157.

54 John Carlson and Neville Yeomans, "Whither Goeth the Law – Humanity or Barbarity," in Margaret Smith and David Crossley, eds., *The Way Out: Radical Alternatives in Australia* (Melbourne: Lansdowne Press, 1975), 155.

55 Charles J. Dunlap Jr., "Lawfare 101: A Primer," *Military Review* (May–June 2017), 9.

Declared 'the newest feature of 21st Century combat,' Dunlap's concept was influenced by the American experience of the Yugoslav Wars in which 'NATO's lawyers ... became in effect, its tactical commanders' given the unprecedented degree to which they were directly involved in managing combat operations.[56] The 'foes of the United States,' in other words, were starting to use international law – and NATO's fear of violating it – to undercut Western power.[57] It is therefore not especially surprising that he couched it narrowly and emphasized its negative connotations.[58] Using law as a weapon of war was restricted to being 'a method of warfare where law is used as a means of realizing a military objective.'[59] It was intended for application to the international law of armed conflict and would be conducted by 'a trained cadre of military lawyers to support combat operations in the field.'[60] Like realpolitik before it, lawfare was seen as a negative development that 'hijacked' the rule of law 'to the detriment of humanitarian values and law itself' and 'too often produces behaviors that jeopardize the protection of the truly innocent.'[61] In short, it was a dastardly tactic employed by weaker enemies to 'handcuff' the US and its allies by tying them down with vexatious litigation, undermining domestic support for their operations, and corroding the American-led rules-based international order.[62]

Dunlap's early negative conception of lawfare was mirrored by the then-US Secretary of Defense, the late Donald Rumsfeld, whose 2005 *National Defense Strategy* warned that 'Our strength as a nation will continue to be challenged by those who employ a strategy of the weak using international fora, judicial processes, and terrorism.'[63] His subsequent memoir, *Known and Unknown* (2011), devotes an entire chapter to 'Law in a Time of War' and elaborates on his earlier statement, defining lawfare as 'a new kind of asymmetric war waged by our enemies' which 'uses international and domestic legal claims, regardless of their factual basis, to win public support to harass American officials – military and civilian – and to score ideological victories.'[64] These 'legal traps' set by enemies abroad and useful idiots at home were 'particularly effective against the US' because they exploited its 'laudable reverence' for law and legal institutions to constrain its ability to

56 Dunlap, "Law and Military Interventions," 2; and Richard K. Betts, "Review Essay: Compromised Command – Inside NATO's First War," Review of Waging Modern War: Bosnia, Kosovo, and the Future of Combat, by Wesley Clark, *Foreign Affairs*, Vol. 80, No. 4 (2001), 130.
57 Dunlap, "Law and Military Interventions," 1–4; and David B. Rivkin Jr. and Lee A. Casey, "The Rocky Shoals of International Law," *The National Interest*, Vol. 62 (Winter 2000/01), 35–45.
58 Kittrie, *Lawfare*, 6.
59 Dunlap, "Law and Military Interventions," 4.
60 Ibid., 11.
61 Ibid., 4.
62 Ibid., 19.
63 Quoted in Kittrie, *Lawfare*, 30.
64 Donald Rumsfeld, *Known and Unknown: A Memoir* (Sentinel Paperback, 2012), 595.

wage war or defend itself like an 'American Gulliver.'[65] Rumsfeld's exceptionally dim view of lawfare 'has been extensively criticized, and rightly so' for likening it to terrorism, treating international law and American security as necessarily incompatible, and dismissing its potential as a devastating weapon in the superpower arsenal.[66]

A very different negative conception of lawfare emerged contemporaneously from critical scholars such as John Comaroff and David Kennedy. Comaroff, in his 2001 essay on 'Colonialism, Culture, and the Law,' denounced the 'lawfare of domination' practiced by the West as a 'mode of warfare' designed to 'conquer and control indigenous peoples by the coercive use of legal means.'[67] Not only could it be used by the strong to suppress the purportedly 'primitive' and 'dangerous' practices of the weak, it could warp the very reality of indigenous peoples by forcibly reordering their legal concepts, institutions, and hierarchies. This was later restated by both John and Jean Comaroff as, variously, a 'Lilliputian Strategy,' 'the resort to legal instruments, to the violence inherent in the law, to commit acts of political coercion, even erasure' and the use of rules by 'imperialism… to impose a sense of order upon its subordinates by means of violence rendered legible, legal, and legitimate by its own sovereign word. And also to commit its own ever-so civilized, patronizing, high-minded forms of kleptocracy.'[68] The Comaroffs note the tendency of superpower lawfare to 'produce its own antithesis' as its victims turn such tactics against their aggressors 'to challenge both old and new hierarchies of power' on their own terms.[69] Ultimately, however, they reiterate their critical pessimism and conclude that the proliferation of lawfare and its judicializing 'culture of legality' can only ever benefit the hegemonic Western international order with all the iniquity and 'structural violence' that it entails.[70]

Kennedy makes similar points in his *Of War and Law* (2006) in which he defines lawfare in conventional terms as both 'the waging of war by law' and 'managing law and war together.'[71] Noting the potential for lawfare to be used both by terrorists and superpowers in asymmetrical conflicts, he doubts that modern law and war can be anything other than the continuation of one

65 Ibid., 595–596.
66 Kittrie, 30.
67 John Comaroff, "Colonialism, Culture, and the Law: A Foreword," *Law and Social Enquiry*, Vol. 26 (2001), 306–307.
68 John Comaroff and Jean Comaroff, "Law and Disorder in the Postcolony: An Introduction" *Social Anthropology*, Vol. 15 (2007), 30.
69 Comaroff, "Colonialism, Culture, and the Law," 306; Comaroff and Comaroff, "Law and Disorder in the Postcolony," 34.
70 Comaroff, "Colonialism, Culture, and the Law," 307; Comaroff and Comaroff, "Law and Disorder in the Postcolony," 27–29; John Comaroff, 'Foreword' to Zanin et al., *Lawfare*, vii.
71 David Kennedy, *Of War and Law* (Princeton, 2006), 12, 125.

another and the unequal political systems driving both.[72] As the 'legalization of warfare' continues apace, meaningful distinctions between war and peace, politics and litigation, decision-making and rule-following, are breaking down with calamitous results for humanitarianism, responsibility, and accountability.[73] These fears are unwittingly near-identical to Rumsfeld's own, 'when lawyers start making decisions for policy-makers or for those on the firing line.'[74] While these critical conceptions of lawfare exerted no direct influence over the future development of lawfare (likely because they are simply too esoteric and labored to be of any practical consequence or worth citing in professional literature), these scholars, writing when they did, had three prescient insights: (1) that lawfare could indeed be wielded by strong Western powers; (2) that, like any new weapon, it would eventually be mastered by the initial victim and turned against the original aggressor; and (3) that, even if it is a regrettable phenomenon, there is a morally ambiguous quality about lawfare which can be used by anybody for good or ill.

All of this anticipated Dunlap's 2008 revisions to his original position as he broadened the conceptual scope of lawfare while jettisoning its putative negative connotations. While Islamists, to the chagrin of many neoconservatives, had long since proven themselves adept at manipulating international and domestic law against Western interests, by this point the US was also starting to wage lawfare more effectively, albeit on an ad hoc basis.[75] Taking all this into account, Dunlap redefined lawfare as 'the strategy of using – or misusing – law as a substitute for traditional military means to achieve an operational objective' which 'is much like a tool or weapon that can be used properly in accordance with the higher virtues of the rule of law – or not.'[76] Although he has since offered a range of slightly different definitions, the core of Dunlap's thought has remained relatively consistent. His own revisions, as well as those of his competitors, are ultimately 'concerned with the instrumentalization or politicization of the law to achieve a tactical, operational or strategic effect.'[77] Thus, in 2016, when Orde F. Kittrie published the only book-length treatment of the subject – *Lawfare: Law as a Weapon of War*

72 Ibid, 13, 46, 113; David Kennedy, "Lawfare and Warfare" in James Crawford and Martti Koskenniemi, eds., *The Cambridge Companion to International Law* (Cambridge, 2012), 160–161.
73 Kennedy, *Of War and Law*, 12.
74 Donald Rumsfeld, *Rumsfeld's Rules: Leadership Lessons in Business, Politics, War, and Life* (Broadside Books, 2013), 207.
75 Kittrie, *Lawfare*, 7; Zoey Kotzambasis, "Lawfare: A New Tool for Fighting Terrorism," *Arizona Journal of International & Comparative Law*, Vol. 35, No. 1 (2018); and Gregory Noone, "Lawfare or Strategic Communications?" Case *Western Reserve Journal of International Law*, Vol. 43, No. 1 (2010).
76 Charles J, Dunlap Jr., "Lawfare Today: A Perspective," *Yale Journal of International Affairs* (Winter 2008), 146–148.
77 Dale Stephens, "The Age of Lawfare," *International Law Studies*, Vol. 87 (2011), 327.

(2016) – he merely reformulated Dunlap's revised definition as a two-stage test:

> (1) the actor uses law to create the same or similar effects as those traditionally sought from conventional kinetic military action – including impacting the key armed force decision-making and capabilities of the target; and (2) one of the actor's motivations is to weaken or destroy an adversary against which the lawfare is being deployed.[78]

This intention-and-effects-based definition was a response to the 'tremendous missed opportunity' that was 'the US government's lack of systematic engagement with lawfare' and its reactive approach to practicing it.[79] While Kittrie followed Dunlap to the extent that he associated lawfare most closely with the state – as practitioner and subject – and active military operations, he broadened its scope beyond international law and the kinetic battlefield. Thus, by recognizing the 'remarkable variety' and 'exceptional creativity' inherent in 'instrumental lawfare,' Kittrie acknowledged that it could be waged with international and domestic law in international and domestic forums.[80] This was indicative of the changing nature of geopolitical conflict up to 2016 as all manner of state and non-state actors seized on law as a means to inflict economic and reputational damage on one another far beyond the battlefront.[81] In short, Kittrie's book was a 'call to action' for Western governments and scholars who continued to neglect this rapidly evolving phenomenon.[82]

Such has been the pace of change, however, that Kittrie's broad conception of lawfare was outdated on arrival. The first sign of this within the scholarly literature can be seen in Siri Gloppen's 2018 paper for the Center of Law and Social Transformation which posits that the 'analytical core' of lawfare is 'the strategic use of rights, law and litigation by actors of different breeds to advance contested political and social goals.'[83] Gloppen perceptively noted that lawfare had become the 'common mode of social and political contestation' in disputes unrelated to conventional military objectives.[84] Many of these were between adaptable networks of actors who mobilized support and

---

78 Kittrie, *Lawfare*, 6–8. This influenced, and is similar to, the definition offered by Joel Trachtman – "legal activity that supports, undermines, or substitutes for other types of warfare," Joel Trachtman, "Integrating Lawfare and Warfare," *Boston College International and Comparative Law Review*, Vol. 39, No. 2 (2016), 268.

79 Kittrie, *Lawfare*, 3, 28–38.

80 Ibid., 11.

81 Ibid., 11–28.

82 Ibid., 3, 10–11, 329.

83 Siri Gloppen, "Conceptualizing Lawfare: A Typology & Theoretical Framework," *Center of Law and Social Transformation* (2018), 6.

84 Ibid., 26.

instrumentalized law to achieve their goals in ideological struggles over identity politics.[85] While she was more concerned with the relevance of lawfare to the 'legalization or judicialization of politics' than its geopolitical application, Gloppen's underlying point remains valid: the practical potential of lawfare now transcends the strict military sphere.[86] As much has been recognized by Jill I. Goldenziel in her 2020 article, 'Law as a Battlefield: The US, China and the Escalation of Lawfare,' which contains the most refined scholarly definition of lawfare to date. In developing it, Goldenziel takes into account the hybridization of modern conflict and the resulting intensification of geopolitical competition in every imaginable sphere from international arbitration to trade regulations to cyberspace. In particular, she emphasizes the importance of 'information lawfare' to messaging and narrative control over conflicts fought in the digital age.[87] Accordingly, she redefines lawfare as:

(1) the purposeful use of law taken toward a particular adversary with the goal of achieving a particular strategic, operational, or tactical objective, or (2) the purposeful use of law to bolster the legitimacy of one's own strategic, operational, or tactical objectives toward a particular adversary, or to weaken the legitimacy of a particular adversary's particular strategic, operational, or tactical objectives.[88]

This goes beyond straightforward offensive/defensive military lawfare operations targeting clearly defined enemies in open conflict to encompass 'shaping the environment' strategies and 'proxy lawfare,' which involves 'taking legal actions using adversary proxies.'[89] While this is a marked improvement on earlier definitions in terms of balancing precision and adaptability, Goldenziel remains firmly wedded to a traditional state-and-military-led lawfare.[90] For example, she confines Western lawfare to the use – not creation – of law

---

85 Ibid., 1–5.
86 Ibid., 2. This has long been appreciated by the authors of the popular Lawfare blog, who refer to "the use of law as a weapon of conflict and, perhaps more importantly, to the depressing reality that America remains at war with itself over the law governing its warfare with others." While they have broadened the definition of lawfare to one that is unworkable in practice, they admit that in titling their blog they used "this latter sense of the word – which is admittedly not its normal usage." See "About," *Lawfare*, September 1, 2010, http://www.lawfareblog.org.
87 Jill I. Goldenziel, "Information Lawfare: Messaging and the Moral High Ground," *Journal of National Security Law & Policy*, Vol. 12 (2021), 795–807.
88 Goldenziel, "Law as a Battlefield," 1087, 1097.
89 Ibid., 1097–1099.
90 This is reflected in the latest French thinking on lawfare as 'the use of law to conduct warfare' and the 'use of [international] law to establish, perpetuate, or change power relations in order to counter an adversary' – Amélie Ferey, *Towards a War of Norms? From Lawfare to Legal Operations* (Focus Stratégique, Ifri, April 2022), 9–10.

by state authorities and proposes a 'central lawfare office' to help civilian agencies coordinate with the military to plan and operationalize it.[91] While her recommendation to institutionalize lawfare is sound, for reasons that will become clear her overall approach is unduly restrictive given contemporary geopolitical conditions. Regardless, Goldenziel is entirely correct in criticizing the 'woefully underdeveloped' and 'haphazard' state of Western strategy and practice.[92] She is also correct to reiterate that overly theoretical, overly elaborate, and overly capacious definitions are 'not analytically useful for academics and impossible to operationalize in the military or policy realm.'[93] Indeed,

> To say that lawfare involves any use of law, or any national security matter, risks a definition too broad to provide useful guidance for policymakers and the military ... To be lawfare, laws and legal actions must be employed with an explicit purpose, against a particular adversary, and to achieve a specific objective.[94]

Regrettably, the most recent lawfare scholarship ignores these necessary limitations and bastardizes the term beyond recognition. For example, in their *Lawfare: Waging War through Law* (2022), Cristiano Zanin, Valeska Martins, and Rafael Valim redefine lawfare as 'the strategic use of law with the purpose of delegitimizing, harming or annihilating an enemy,'[95] while Jaume Castan Pinos and Mark Friis Hau's *Lawfare: New Trajectories in Law* (2023) provides an even more generic conception of lawfare as 'a multifaceted law-based instrument that can be used by a wide range of actors in both military and non-military contexts to pursue political objectives.'[96] The former authors are Brazilian lawyers writing in the context of their country's fraught domestic politics to advance – with a foreword by John Comaroff – a 'critical view' in defense of President Lula against the 'villainy' of ultra-politicized litigation and abuses of process.[97] The latter duo are writing – also with an endorsement by Comaroff – as critical sociologists with the intention of providing a 'deliberately inclusive new conceptualization' and typology that recognize the 'polysemantic and complex nature' of the term in contrast to 'the dominant military-grounded definition.'[98] Both contributions are right to highlight the paucity of serious scholarship on the theory and intellectual

91 Ibid., 1096, 1099, 1164.
92 Ibid., 1090, 1171.
93 Goldenziel, "Law as a Battlefield," 1096.
94 Goldenziel, "Information Lawfare," 798–799.
95 Zanin et al. *Lawfare*, 4.
96 Pinos and Hau, *Lawfare*, 2.
97 Zanin et al. *Lawfare*, 4, 81.
98 Pinos and Hau, *Lawfare*, Blurb and 2.

foundations of lawfare, and each highlights many interesting examples of potential lawfare tactics in various contexts while illustrating their corrosive effects on democracies under the rule of law if left unchecked. Crucially, however, neither conceptualization possesses a stable analytical core capable of distinguishing it from mundane litigation launched against any opponent by anyone for any personal, politicized, or strategic purpose. In short, these new critical definitions fail Goldenziel's requirement that they remain taut enough for practical use in the field.

That contemporary lawfare scholarship should revert to its mid-2000s critical phase is especially unfortunate given that the term is exploding into everyday usage and undergoing rapid banalization as a result. At the time of writing, in December 2023, a Google search for 'lawfare' returned well over three million results (double the number for July 2020) while the Google Books Ngram Viewer reveals a huge surge of appearances in printed sources from the 2010s onward.[99] For example, its first appearance in a reputable English dictionary occurred in 2022 when Collins' Dictionary defined it as 'the strategic use of legal proceedings to intimidate or hinder an opponent.'[100] Similarly, in 2023 the eminent human rights barrister, Geoffrey Robertson KC, published a trade book titled *Lawfare* in which he describes it as a 'weak pun with a pejorative tinge' which 'has come to mean the use of legal strategies to harass and intimidate publishers' via Strategic [Defamation] Lawsuits Against Public Participation (SLAPP) brought by 'Russians, the Rich and the Government.'[101]

Beyond these mainstream publications, 'lawfare' is being thrown about with even less precision and ever greater abandon. For example, it has recently been used by various scholars to describe politicized legal pluralism and forum-shopping in postwar Chechnya, acrimonious constitutional litigation in South Africa, and, more generally, 'the weaponization of national judicial systems by political parties to delegitimize, harass, bankrupt, disqualify, and sometimes imprison politicians of other parties.'[102] This is broadly what

---

99 See Zanin et al. vii; Pinos and Hau, 4.
100 "Definition of Lawfare," *Collins English Dictionary*, accessed October 23, 2023, https://www.collinsdictionary.com/dictionary/english/lawfare.
101 Geoffrey Robertson KC, *Lawfare* (TLS Books, 2023), 2–3. See also the rudimentary and confused understandings of lawfare in "Lawfare and the UK Court System," *House of Commons Research Briefing*, January 19, 2022, https://commonslibrary.parliament.uk/research-briefings/cdp-2022-0016/.
102 Egor Lazarev, *State-Building as Lawfare: Custom, Sharia, and State Law in Postwar Chechnya* (Cambridge: Cambridge University Press, 2023); Dennis Davis and Michelle Le Roux, *Lawfare: Judging Politics in South Africa* (Jonathan Ball Publishing, 2019); Kate Dent, *Lawfare and Judicial Legitimacy: The Judicialisation of Politics in the Case of South Africa* (Routledge, 2023); Michael Lind, "Our Weaponized Legal System Misfires," *Tablet Magazine*, May 16, 2023, https://www.tabletmag.com/sections/news/articles/our-weaponized-legal-system-misfires.

Pope Francis meant when in 2019 he denounced lawfare as a mass media populist phenomenon involving 'exogeneous intervention in the political scenarios of countries [i.e. Brazil] through the misuse of legal procedures and legal classifications.'[103] Although these examples could conceivably amount to lawfare if they satisfied Goldenziel's tests, on the face of it there is nothing to distinguish them from routine political litigation that has characterized internal democratic squabbles since the time of Classical Athens. In other words, these are potential lawfare tactics, but they are not definitive of lawfare properly so-called which requires, at the very least, a geopolitical conflict, adversary, and strategic objective.

If this classical (i.e. Dunlap/Kittrie/Goldenziel) understanding of lawfare is applied anachronistically, Western nations have been engaging in intentional acts of lawfare since the Dutch East India Company commissioned Hugo Grotius to write *Mare Liberum* (1609) with a view to justifying attacks on their Portuguese rivals on the high seas.[104] In more recent times, the tendency has been to focus on 'battlefield-exploitation lawfare,' meaning the leveraging of an enemy's compliance with international and/or humanitarian law to gain battlefield advantages.[105] This typically involves attempts to win propaganda victories and undermine public will on the home front by portraying the enemy as an aggressor and violator of human rights so that they impose greater self-restraint and become less effective in combat.[106] Examples of this type of lawfare include defending against Taliban propaganda and litigation arising from their use of civilian human shields (itself a violation of the law of armed conflict) to discourage NATO airstrikes, via the US government's imposition of sanctions against the Iraqi Air Force prior to the Second Gulf War which prevented it acquiring any new aircraft or parts, to the UK's Overseas Operations (Service Personnel and Veterans) Act 2021 which seeks to protect service personnel and veterans from vexatious legal action relating to overseas operations.[107] Instances of 'instrumental lawfare,' meaning the substitution of legal tools for kinetic weaponry to achieve military objectives, are also becoming more common and varied.[108] Examples of this type of lawfare are virtually unlimited and include everything from Israel's leveraging of maritime

103 Quoted in Zanin et al., 4 and Eduardo Campos Lima, "Francis causes controversy in Brazil for saying Lula was victim of lawfare," *Crux*, April 4, 2023, https://cruxnow.com/church-in -the-americas/2023/04/francis-causes-controversy-in-brazil-for-saying-lula-was-victim-of -lawfare.
104 Kittrie, *Lawfare* 4–5.
105 Goldenziel, "Law as a Battlefield," 1095. Also known more cumbersomely as "compliance-leverage disparity lawfare" – see Kittrie, *Lawfare*, 11.
106 Kittrie, *Lawfare*, 18.
107 Ibid., 7, 18–28; Goldenziel, "Law as a Battlefield," 1095; and "Overseas Operations (Service Personnel and Veterans) Bill 2019–2021: Lords amendments," *House of Commons Research Briefing*, April 27, 2021, https://commonslibrary.parliament.uk/research-briefings/cbp-9198.
108 Kittrie, *Lawfare*, 11; and Goldenziel, "Law as a Battlefield," 1094.

insurance companies to prevent flotillas from reaching Gaza, to the US government imposing financial sanctions against the Iranian regime.[109] While all of this suggests that the West is at least dimly conscious of the potential of lawfare and does sometimes employ it, it remains difficult to measure the cumulative success of such efforts precisely because they are isolated incidents.

Despite the UK's longstanding (and reasonably successful) ambition to become 'lawyer and adviser to the world,'[110] lawfare is simply listed as one of the responsibilities of the Parliamentary Under-Secretary of State for Justice (a junior minister in the Ministry of Justice), and, excepting the revocation of maritime insurance for a Russian supply ship bound for Syria in 2012, most of the attention has been narrowly focused on the use of human rights legislation against soldiers and libel suits against journalists.[111] Despite a 2020 speech by the then-Chief of Defence Staff warning of the sophistication of Chinese lawfare,[112] the term 'lawfare' was absent entirely from the UK's 2021 *Integrated Review of Security, Defence, Development and Foreign Policy*,[113] is referenced only once in the Ministry of Defence's (MoD) 2021 *Integrated Operating Concept 2025* as a potential 'support [for] conventional military operations,'[114] and appears twice in a single paragraph in the MoD's 2022 *UK*

109 Kittrie, *Lawfare*, 12–17.
110 Kenneth Clarke KC, "Kenneth Clarke: UK should be lawyer and adviser to the world," *UK Government Press Release*, September 14, 2011, https://www.gov.uk/government/news/kenneth-clarke-uk-should-be-lawyer-and-adviser-to-the-world; "Legal Services are GREAT," *UK Government Press Release*, October 5, 2017, https://www.gov.uk/government/news/legal-services-are-great; Antonia Romeo, "How legal exports are powering the UK economy," *Prospect Magazine*, December 1, 2020, https://www.prospectmagazine.co.uk/economics-and-finance/how-legal-exports-are-powering-the-uk-economy; and Nick Cohen, "Export-only Justice," *The Spectator*, December 8, 2020, https://www.spectator.co.uk/article/export-only-justice.
111 Kittrie, *Lawfare*, 2; "Ministerial role: Parliamentary Under Secretary of State," *Ministry of Justice*, accessed October 23, 2023, https://www.gov.uk/government/ministers/parliamentary-under-secretary-of-state--108; *Legal Protections for Armed Forces Personnel and Veterans serving in operations outside the United Kingdom*, (Ministry of Defence, July 22, 2019), https://assets.publishing.service.gov.uk/government/uploads/system/uploads/attachment_data/file/919822/20190718-MOD_consultation_document-FINAL.pdf; and HC Deb, (October 17, 2022) vol. 720 cols. 497–506 (UK).
112 General Sir Nick Carter, "Chief of the Defence Staff, General Sir Nick Carter launches the Integrated Operating Concept" (Speech, London, September 30, 2020), Ministry of Defence, https://www.gov.uk/government/speeches/chief-of-the-defence-staff-general-sir-nick-carter-launches-the-integrated-operating-concept.
113 *Global Britain in a competitive age: The Integrated Review of Security, Defence, Development and Foreign Policy*, (U.K. Cabinet Office, March 16, 2021), https://www.gov.uk/government/publications/global-britain-in-a-competitive-age-the-integrated-review-of-security-defence-development-and-foreign-policy/global-britain-in-a-competitive-age-the-integrated-review-of-security-defence-development-and-foreign-policy.
114 *Strategic Operating Concept 2025* (Ministry of Defence, August 2021), 5–6, https://assets.publishing.service.gov.uk/government/uploads/system/uploads/attachment_data/file/1014659/Integrated_Operating_Concept_2025.pdf.

Defence Doctrine in a largely defensive context as a 'military instrument' that 'can be used by adversary states to undermine the legitimacy of the UK government's position directly, or by civil society proxies through vexatious litigation to prevent or slow activities.'[115]

The only relevant US institutions are ancillary appendages of the State and Justice departments. First, the Office of the Legal Adviser to the State Department has a broad remit to furnish advice 'on all legal issues, domestic and international, arising in the course of the Department's work' such as treaties, international law, and foreign policy.[116] It employs 300 permanent staff including 200 attorneys and is organized into functional and regional sections to provide specialized legal support to each of the State Department's internal bureaus.[117] Second is the fairly obscure Office of Foreign Litigation (OFL) which exists 'to ensure that the United States' wide range of policies, programs, and activities are fully protected when challenged through foreign court litigation.'[118] It safeguards 'U.S. interests in all litigation pending in foreign courts, whether civil or criminal, affirmative or defensive' by, for example, instructing foreign counsel and advising other branches of government involved with proceedings in foreign jurisdictions.[119] However, 'most Office of Foreign Litigation cases are defensive,' and there is nothing by way of systematized lawfare – no office, no manpower, no resources, no strategy of any sort.[120] Most lawfare-type activity has been carried out by private citizens and NGOs, with some states and cities supporting their campaigns or adopting their tactics against US adversaries; the executive branch, however, has been 'frozen into much the same largely defensive crouch where it was in 2005' under Rumsfeld's Department of Defense.[121]

Israel and Ukraine are alone among Western nations in having dedicated lawfare institutions and personnel. The former has a Military Advocate General (MAG) Corps with around 60 'military legal experts whose job is to justify the legality of the use of force' and 'exploiting the grey areas of international law in order to allow the IDF free rein.'[122] Israel also has a lawfare

115 *UK Defence Doctrine*, 6th ed. (Ministry of Defence, November 2022), 28, https://assets.publishing.service.gov.uk/government/uploads/system/uploads/attachment_data/file/1118720/UK_Defence_Doctrine_Ed6.pdf.

116 "Office of the Legal Adviser," *U.S Department of State*, accessed December 28, 2023, https://www.state.gov/bureaus-offices/secretary-of-state/office-of-the-legal-adviser/.

117 "About Us – Legal Adviser," *U.S Department of State*, accessed December 28, 2023, https://www.state.gov/about-us-legal-adviser/.

118 "Office of Foreign Litigation," *U.S Department of Justice*, accessed October 23, 2023, https://www.justice.gov/civil/office-foreign-litigation.

119 Ibid.

120 Ibid; Goldenziel, "Law as a Battlefield," 1090; and Kittrie, *Lawfare*, 28, 160.

121 Kittrie, *Lawfare*, 28–33.

122 Amélie Ferey, *Towards a War of Norms? From Lawfare to Legal Operations*, 25.

office in its Ministry of Justice and a public-private partnership with the Shurat HaDin Law Center (an NGO) which operates worldwide to assist in 'bankrupting terror groups and grinding their activity to a halt.'[123] However, even these are largely limited, defensive measures, as the Israeli government has been reluctant both to publicize novel tactics and to set precedents 'that could be used against it by its adversaries.'[124] The limits of Israeli lawfare capabilities recently became apparent in the aftermath of the October 7, 2023, atrocities perpetrated by Hamas, the Gaza-based terrorist organization which habitually uses extreme violence in combination with information lawfare as 'a central tenet of their strategy.'[125] As Dunlap notes, Hamas' aggressive use of provocation, denial, and disinformation to sour global public opinion against Israel required, but was not met with, a rapid, systematic response combining strict rhetorical discipline, detailed rebuttals to mis/disinformation, and an ongoing campaign to educate the IDF and the world about Hamas' cynical lawfare techniques.[126] Such failings are by no means total or unique to Israel: it has mounted a rigorous defense against malicious allegations of genocide brought by South Africa at the International Court of Justice (ICJ), while 'poor interagency coordination stymies the U.S. government's response to disinformation, and renders long-term, proactive information campaigns nearly impossible.'[127] In short, Israel's lawfare capabilities remain deficient, but they are still more robust than those of their most advanced Western allies.

By contrast, Ukraine 'proudly advertises its Lawfare Project on its government website' and classifies it as a branch of hybrid warfare designed to 'harm Russia's reputation in the international community and give states legal ammunition to sanction Russia.'[128] Launched in 2014 in the aftermath of the Russian invasion of Crimea, the Lawfare Project team has brought 'lawsuits under both public and private international law' through the Ministry of Foreign Affairs and Ministry of Justice.[129] The Ukrainian government appears

123 Goldenziel, "Law as a Battlefield," 1090; Kittrie, *Lawfare*, 311–312.

124 Kittrie, *Lawfare*, 311.

125 Charles J, Dunlap Jr., "Five ideas to counter Hamas' lawfare strategy…and why," *Lawfire*, October 15, 2023, https://sites.duke.edu/lawfire/2023/10/15/five-ideas-to-counter-hamas-lawfare-strategy-and-why/.

126 Ibid.

127 Natasha Hausdorff, "The International Court of Justice has been weaponised against the Jewish state," *The Telegraph*, January 7, 2024, https://www.telegraph.co.uk/news/2024/01/07/international-court-of-justice-weaponised-against-jewish/; Jill I. Goldenziel and Daniel Grant, "Information Resilience: Countering Disinformation and its Threat to the U.S. Alliance System," *War on the Rocks*, November 15, 2023, https://warontherocks.com/2023/11/information-resilience-countering-disinformation-and-its-threat-to-the-u-s-alliance-system/.

128 Jill I. Goldenziel, "An Alternative to Zombieing: Lawfare between Russia and Ukraine and the Future of International Law," *Cornell Law Review*, Vol. 108 (2022), 1–2.

129 "Teams," *Law Confrontation with Russian Federation*, accessed October 23, 2023, https://lawfare.gov.ua/teams.

to also be coordinating claims by Ukrainian state-owned institutions, utilizing investor-state dispute settlement (ISDS) to claim billions from Russia, and has expressly encouraged private investors to follow their example.[130] The project has

> generated landmark legal rulings and victories – including an ICJ order for Russia to cease hostilities, isolation of Russia in the World Trade Organization (WTO), two victories in the International Tribunal for the Law of the Sea (ITLOS), and $8 billion in arbitration damages.[131]

Its effectiveness has convincingly demonstrated 'the need for the state to have a centralized legal strategy' with specialized institutions and personnel capable of planning, coordinating, and executing lawfare campaigns.[132] While enforcing judgments against Russia is 'notoriously difficult,' early awards have proved enforceable, and they can still be enforced in jurisdictions where Russia has assets not protected by immunity.[133] Additionally, by publicly broadcasting the decisions, the judgments are effective information lawfare tools that promote Ukraine's narrative, delegitimize Russia's actions, and bolster international efforts to sanction Russia.[134]

On the global stage, the Office of the Legal Advisor at NATO's Supreme Headquarters Allied Powers Europe (SHAPE) has some staff dedicated to defensive 'Legal Operations' around battlefield scenarios under international law.[135] Tellingly, officials from the organization rarely refer to 'lawfare,' and one has explicitly rejected the term 'lawfare' because it is seen

130 PrivatBank, *Law Confrontation with Russian Federation*, accessed October 23, 2023, https://lawfare.gov.ua/teams/privatbank; Naftogaz, *Law Confrontation with Russian Federation*, accessed October 23, 2023; "Oschadbank Files Claim Worth UAH 15 Bln Against Russia for Losses Caused by Crimean Annexation – Yatseniuk," *Interfax-Ukraine*, August 7, 2015, https://en.interfax.com.ua/news/economic/276618.html.
131 Goldenziel, "An Alternative to Zombieing," 1–2.
132 Zakhar Tropin, "Lawfare as part of hybrid wars: The experience of Ukraine in conflict with Russian Federation," *Security and Defence Quarterly*, No. 1 (2021), 15–29.
133 Ibid. 10.
134 Eric Chang, "Lawfare in Ukraine: Weaponizing International Investment Law and the Law of Armed Conflict Against Russia's Invasion," *Strategic Perspectives*, No. 39 (INSS, August 2022), 18.
135 Goldenziel, "Law as a Battlefield," 1090; Major General Barre R. Seguin, "The Use Of Legal Operations in a Context of Hybrid Threats and Strategic Competition," (Speech, Washington, D. C., published March 13, 2020), *Lawfire*, https://sites.duke.edu/lawfire/2020/03/13/a-warfighters-perspective-on-lawfare-in-an-era-of-hybrid-threats-and-strategic-competition; and Andrés Muñoz Mosquera and Sascha-Dominik Bachmann, "Understanding Lawfare in a Hybrid Warfare Context," *NATO Legal Gazette*, No. 37 (October 2016), 5–23.

as 'less comprehensive, more limited in scope, and the object of academic controversies.'[136] Instead, NATO uses the term 'legal operations' to denote:

> the use of law as an instrument of power. The term encompasses any actions in the legal domain by state or non-state actors aimed at, among others, gaining – or undermining the opponent's – legitimacy, advancing interests, or enhancing/denying capabilities, at the tactical, operational, strategic and/or (geo)political levels. Legal operations may be used across the whole peace-crisis-conflict spectrum through and in combination with a wide range of DIMEFIL tools, not necessarily of a legal nature.[137]

Terminology aside, it is evident that NATO's Office of Legal Affairs recognizes the pressing need to develop its hybrid capabilities in 'fluid' legal environments such as outer space in order to secure 'influence' and 'objects of desire' without resort to kinetic force.[138] Even so, its nascent Defence Innovation Accelerator for the North Atlantic (DIANA) – essentially a funding body and test center network to support start-ups that produce dual-use technologies for the Alliance – does not classify law as a technology for investment purposes, meaning lawfare is effectively excluded from the program's scope.[139] Across the broader private sector there are still no firms – law or defense – dedicated solely or substantially to lawfare, with the most specialized firms being boutique multi-service partnerships.[140] Twenty years and numerous lost wars after Dunlap's paper, then, there is still no coherent tradition, no accepted doctrine, no established practice, no coordination, no widespread interest, no advanced institutionalization, and no private industry. All of this would suggest that Western lawfare has shallow roots, an unstable but serviceable portmanteau unconnected to any established traditions of thought. The same certainly cannot be said for its most dangerous counterpart.

---

136 Rodrigo Vázquez Benítez, "Legal Operations: The Use of Law as an Instrument of Power in the Context of Hybrid Threats and Strategic Competition," NATO Legal Gazette, No. 41 (2020), 141.

137 Ibid., 140.

138 Borja Montes Toscano, Andrés Muñoz Mosquera, "Space Domain, Autonomous Warfare and Hybrid Environments: The next challenges for NATO," *NATO Legal Gazette*, No. 42 (2021), 12.

139 "Challenges," *NATO Defence Innovation Accelerator for the North Atlantic (DIANA)*, accessed October 23, 2023, https://www.diana.nato.int/challenges.html.

140 See, for example, "About," *McCue Jury & Partners*, accessed October 23, 2023, https://www.mccue-law.com/about/; "Lawfare strategist Jason McCue goes into battle for Ukraine," *Intelligence Online*, July 12, 2023, https://www.intelligenceonline.com/corporate-intelligence/2023/07/12/lawfare-strategist-jason-mccue-goes-into-battle-for-ukraine,110002701-art.

2 The Chinese Way of Unrestricted Lawfare

2.1 The Strategic Tradition

The Chinese have 'taken a greater interest in their history – and for longer – than any other civilization.'[1] As well they might, for theirs can claim to be the oldest continuous civilization on earth. It began in chaos, not creationism. Far back in the realm of myth, 'all was vague and amorphous' until the 'Great Beginning' simply happened as heaven and earth drifted apart.[2] Only then did the industrious gods intervene, working in concert to calculate the dimensions of time and space, divide up the elements, and maintain the correct functioning of all things under heaven.[3] Order and stratification, then, are China itself, which, since ancient times, has been 'first and foremost a technical civilization.'[4] Emerging from prehistory within its cradle around the Yellow River basin in the second millennium BC, early Chinese civilization coalesced around writing, the dynastic state, and warfare.[5] Proving adept at all three, the ancient Chinese acquired a distinctive culture with peculiar modes of thought. Like the primordial gods before them, the classical scholars found themselves surrounded by chaos and set about imposing order on their world.

The Golden Age of Chinese philosophy (6th–3rd centuries BC) was a centuries-long era of extremely violent, 'absolute insecurity' during which itinerant scholars took their Hundred Schools of Thought around the myriad warring states vying for dominance over the Chinese heartlands.[6] A dazzling cast of intellects and their great works inspired enduring traditions – Confucianism,

1 John Keay, *China: A History* (London: Harper Press, 2009), 3.
2 Ibid., 25.
3 Ibid., 26.
4 Jacques Gernet, *A History of Chinese Civilisation*, 2 vols., 2nd ed. (London: Folio Society, 1996), 26.
5 Keay, *China*, 11; and Roel Sterckx, *Chinese Thought from Confucius to Cook Ding* (New Orleans: Pelican, 2020), 5.
6 William Jenner, *The Tyranny of History* (London: Penguin, 1994), 20; and Michael Wood, *The Story of China: A Portrait of a Civilisation and its People* (New York: Simon & Schuster, 2020), 73–74.

DOI: 10.4324/9781032724003-2

which emphasized ethical conduct and orderly government; Daoism, which stressed spiritual cultivation and harmonious living; and Legalism, with its exacting standards and all-encompassing legal system[7] – and the forging of an imperial 'singularity' under the First Emperor of Qin, essentially a 'civilization pretending to be a nation-state.'[8] All of this was consolidated for posterity by a burgeoning historical tradition centered upon Sima Tan (d. 110 BC) and Sima Qian (d. 86 BC), whose *Records of the Grand Historian* documented the philosophical, political, and biographical monuments of China down to the 1st century BC.[9] In short, the historical and intellectual experience of the classical period set the mold for subsequent Chinese history and gave rise to a consistent, albeit sometimes contradictory, geopolitical outlook.

The key to the Chinese worldview is its scale. Western visitors since Marco Polo have been struck by the sheer size and splendor of China, the prosperity of its provinces, its technological marvels, and the vitality of its people.[10] The Chinese were themselves conscious of all this, proudly so, and imperial nomenclature broadcasts both the breadth of their ambitions and depth of their self-regard. Emperors of the 'Celestial Empire' or 'Middle Kingdom' or 'Central State' ruled under the Mandate of Heaven as Sons of Heaven, presiding over the Celestial Court to ensure that justice was done for 'all under heaven' through the correct alignment of heavenly reason, state law, and harmonious social relations.[11] For millennia, the affairs of men were so ordered, turning in great cycles like the celestial bodies, as the heavenly mandate passed between dynasties under the 'eyes of heaven.'[12] Even today the flag of the People's Republic of China (PRC) is adorned with five golden stars representing the unity of the Chinese people under the leadership of the CCP led by a leader for life; even today, Chinese nationalism remains suspended in a romanticized constellation of geographic continuity, Han ethnic identity, and a coherent cultural canon.[13] From this cosmic societal vision arose the characteristic Sinocentrism of Chinese foreign policy and an abiding fear of internal disorder within the body politic.

---

7 See Sterckx, *Chinese Thought from Confucius to Cook Ding*, 73–74, 109–110, 125–126.

8 Lucian Pye quoted in Henry Kissinger, *On China* (London: Penguin, 2012), 11.

9 Sterckx, *Chinese Thought from Confucius to Cook Ding*, 7; and Sima Qian, *The First Emperor: Selections from the Historical Records* (Oxford: Oxford University Press, 2007).

10 Kissinger, *On China*, 12.

11 Sterckx, *Chinese Thought from Confucius to Cook Ding*, 4; Kissinger, *On China*, 10.

12 Xiaoqun Xu, *Heaven Has Eyes: A History of Chinese Law* (Oxford: Oxford University Press, 2020), 1. Note the symmetrical opening and closing of Luo Guanzong, Romance of the Three Kingdoms: A Historical Novel, Complete and Unabridged, trans. Moss Roberts, 2 Vols., (Berkeley: University of California Press, 2004) – ("The empire, long divided, must unite; long united, must divide,"), 1; and ("The empire, long united, must divide, and long divided, must unite,"), 935.

13 Youngmin Kim, *A History of Chinese Political Thought* (Cambridge: Polity, 2018), 6–7; Bill Hayton, *The Invention of China* (New Haven: Yale University Press, 2020).

In many respects, Sinocentrism is alien to the universalism of modern Western thought. Unlike the semi-conscious process of Americanization and its ancient predecessor, Romanization, Sinocentrism neither equates to nor requires the Sinofication of non-Chinese societies. Rather, it simply takes for granted that China is the center of the universe and that every 'barbarian' on the world stage, whether supplicant ally or 'foreign devil,' must be managed into its correct orbit as a greater or lesser subordinate.[14] This world system – *tianxia* – is so fundamental to Chinese thought that the 'polity constantly and inevitably feels discontent and insecure without it.'[15] The main task of statesmanship is not, therefore, to convert others to 'Chineseness' or even to spread Chinese culture around the globe – it is to ensure that China retains its natural place as the center of geopolitical gravity by playing rivals off against one another and consolidating its own military might. Foreign policy conducted on this basis manifests in one of two ways throughout Chinese history.[16] In some periods – notably under the later Qing dynasty and Mao's dictatorship – China has turned inwards and isolated itself from an outside world with nothing to offer. This has sometimes proved inconsequential, sometimes prudent, and sometimes disastrous when China has been humiliated and overrun by confederations of foreign enemies. In other periods – notably under the early Tang dynasty and now under Xi Jinping – China has cast its gaze outwards, expanded aggressively, and opened itself up to receive ideas, religions, and riches from abroad.[17] Again, this has sometimes proved inconsequential, sometimes disastrous, and is currently proving highly successful across Africa and Central Asia.

---

14 See Kim, *A History of Chinese Political Thought*, 140–144; and, for detailed historical overviews of Sinocentrism during different periods, see Harry G. Gelber, *The Dragon and the Foreign Devils: China and the World, 1100BC to the Present* (London: Bloomsbury, 2007); Odd Arne Westad, *Restless Empire: China and the World Since 1750* (New York: Vintage, 2013); and Timothy Brook, *Great State: China and the World* (London: Profile, 2021).

15 Fei-Ling Wang quoted in Bret Austin White, "Reordering the Law for a China World Order: China's Legal Warfare Strategy in Outer Space and Cyberspace," *Journal of National Security Law & Policy*, Vol. 11, No. 2 (2021), 442.

16 For a range of historical examples to illustrate these points, see Kissinger, *On China*, 5–22.

17 This is a theme explored in one of the four classical Chinese novels from the 16th century, see Wu Cheng'en, *The Monkey King: Journey to the West* (London: Penguin Classics, 2021). That said, however, foreign ideas and religions are now only embraced to the extent that they complement rather than threaten existing philosophical traditions – see Benedict Rogers, "China Is Already Breaking Its Vatican Deal," *Foreign Policy*, September 17, 2020, https://foreignpolicy .com/2020/09/17/china-francis-vatican. This is also the impression one gets from Michael Sandel's unexpected popularity across China – see Michael J. Sandel and Paul J. D'Ambrosio, eds., *Encountering China: Michael Sandel and Chinese Philosophy* (Cambridge, Mass.: Harvard University Press, 2018). Even socialism is to be imbued with "Chinese characteristics." See also "Xi Jinping's Thought on Socialism with Chinese Characteristics for a New era," *edX Course*, https://www.edx.org/course/xi-jinpings-thought-on-socialism-with-chinese-char.

In contrast with Europe, 'a continent covered with ruins testifying to the fallibility of human foresight,' China has historically been far more concerned with chaos than collapse.[18] While barbarian invaders extinguished Roman civilization, those who overran Chinese territory were only ever subsumed into its existing cultural and bureaucratic rhythms – China itself always endures. Yet Chinese disasters, natural or manmade or both, are typically mass casualty events without parallel. To give just a few examples, China has endured six of the world's ten deadliest natural disasters including the 1931 Yangtze flood which killed upwards of four million people and five of the world's ten bloodiest conflicts including the Taiping Rebellion (1850–64) which claimed around thirty million lives.[19] Such catastrophes were presaged and compounded by chronic mismanagement and incompetence, political corruption and injustice, and surging civil unrest and banditry, and acted as a magnet for foreign incursions or takeovers.[20] Domestic chaos was thus not unreasonably associated with the passing of the Mandate of Heaven and the fall of the ruling class, hence the perennial concern of China's rulers to avert it. This ancient fear has outlasted the empire itself, with corruption being cast as an existential threat by the CCP which is equally adamant about non-interference in its 'internal affairs,' a doctrine of national sovereignty frequently invoked to deflect international criticism of its domestic policies.[21] Again, this is a sensible reading of history for popular disenchantment and the failure of the Sinocentric system against united enemies have unleashed rebellion, invasion, and carnage right across mainland China time and again.[22] It is entirely unsurprising, then, that in response to their historical experience, the Chinese have cultivated one of the richest strategic traditions known to mankind.

As with everything else, modern Chinese strategy rests upon ancient foundations. The Seven Military Classics, of which Sun Tzu's *Art of War* (5th century BC) is the greatest and best known, instructed generations of Chinese

---

18 Kissinger quoted in Niall Ferguson, "The Meaning of Kissinger: A Realist Reconsidered," *Foreign Affairs*, Vol. 94, No. 5 (September/October 2015), 137–138.

19 See, respectively, Chris Courtney, *The Nature of Disaster in China: The 1931 Yangzi River Flood* (Cambridge, 2018), 249; and Wood, *The Story of China*, 414.

20 The theme of another great historical Chinese novel from the 14th century – see Shi Nai'an, *The Water Margin: Outlaws of the Marsh* (North Clarendon, Vt.: Tuttle Classics, 2010).

21 James Leung, "Xi's Corruption Crackdown: How Bribery and Graft Threaten the Chinese Dream," *Foreign Affairs*, Vol. 94, No. 3 (May/June 2015), 32–38; and Kissinger, *World Order*, 229–230.

22 For accounts of some of the most dramatic examples, see Anonymous, *Records of the Three Kingdoms in Plain Language*, trans. Wilt L. Idema and Stephen H. West, (Indianapolis: Hackett, 2016); Stephen Platt, *Imperial Twilight: The Opium War and the End of China's Last Golden Age* (London: Atlantic, 2018); and *Autumn in the Heavenly Kingdom: China, The West and the Epic Story of the Taiping Civil War* (London: Atlantic, 2012); and David J. Silbey, *The Boxer Rebellion and the Great Game in China* (New York: Hill & Wang, 2013).

strategists before they were formally canonized in 1078 AD.[23] Despite its misleading title, this anthology is not straightforwardly a military manual in the Western mold but rather a treatise on strategy itself. *The Art of War* is 'much more powerful' read in this way for it 'lends itself to infinite applications' in sport, business, and everyday life.[24] Positing that wily stratagems are a surer path to victory than brute force, it rapidly acquired a global following once translated into English in 1910 and remains beloved of generals, entrepreneurs, and celebrities the world over.[25] Crucially, however, it feeds and fits within a wider Chinese literary tradition of holistic thought which manifests in myriad guides to leadership, seduction, and sex.[26] Even the superlative Chinese novel – Luo Guanzhong's 14th-century historical epic, *Romance of the Three Kingdoms* – is a 'vernacular expression of Master Sun's ideas,' a 'folk manual for waging war, a description of the classical strategic and tactical solutions.'[27] Much the same is true for China's most successful living author, Mai Jai (Jiang Benhu), who writes wildly popular spy-thrillers and counts Xi Jinping as his number one fan.[28] This cultural mode is merely the finest expression of a strategic language that frames efficacy in terms of transformation and manipulation (instead of decisive action and direct confrontation) and rewards subtlety and evasion (over wanton risk-taking and destruction).[29] Perhaps unsurprisingly, it has provoked admiration, frustration, and disgust among Western commentators for centuries.[30] Regardless, all this translates into geopolitics as *wei qi* (or 'go'), the ancient 'game of surrounding pieces' and multifaceted maneuver for advantage, rather than as the

---

23 See *The Seven Military Classics of Ancient China*, trans. Ralph D. Sawyer (Boulder, Colo.: Westview Press, 1993), 1.

24 Sterckx, *Chinese Thought from Confucius to Cook Ding*, 97; John Minford, introduction to Sun Tzu, *The Art of War* (London: Penguin Classics, 2014), x.

25 Sterckx, *Chinese Thought from Confucius to Cook Ding*, 98; Christopher Andrew, *The Secret World: A History of Intelligence* (London: Allen Lane, 2018), 66–68.

26 For more examples, see Minford, introduction to *The Art of War*, xxix–xxxvii; and Chinghua Tang, *The Ruler's Guide: China's Greatest Emperor and His Timeless Secrets of Success* (Gloucestershire, U.K.: Amberley Publishing, 2017).

27 John Minford, introduction to *The Art of War*, xi.

28 Christopher Andrew and Julius Green, *Stars and Spies: Intelligence Operations and the Entertainment Business* (London: Bodley Head, 2021), 356–357.

29 On this see Francois Jullien, *Detour and Access: Strategies of Meaning in China and Greece* (Princeton: Zone Books, 2004); and *Treatise on Efficacy: Between Western and Chinese Thinking* (Honolulu: University of Hawaii Press, 2004).

30 See, for example, Minford, introduction to *The Art of* War, ix ('beautiful and chilling'); James Murdoch quoted in Minford, introduction to *The Art of War*, xlii – ('the dirtiest form of statecraft with unspeakable depths of duplicity'); and He Xin quoted in Minford, introduction to *The Art of War* xliii – ('We make laws in order to break them; our rules and regulations are a sham. Our tactics consist in carrying out policy; our strategy is to get people to fall into the traps they have set for others.').

more linear game of chess with its emphasis on decisive battle and absolute victory.[31]

In practical terms, this means Chinese geopolitical strategy is farther sighted, far better integrated, and far less compartmentalized than its Western counterparts, with games being played within games within the ultimate game for a Sinocentric world.[32] It is also far more aggressive. As Simon Schama remarked of their antecedent, Communist revolutions are 'powered by brutality,' and Mao's was the most operatically brutal of all.[33] While regime terror has become less frenetic and flagrant since Mao's death, it is no less integral to the ideology and arsenal of today's CCP.[34] Indeed, the threat of violence is now so refined and pervasive that it resembles 'not so much a man-eating tiger or fire-snorting dragon as a giant anaconda coiled in an overhead chandelier.'[35] Accordingly, while the CCP works to expand China's financial and kinetic clout, it is investing heavily in unconventional, cyber, and hybrid capabilities designed to soften up its adversaries as a prelude to '*Wolf Warrior* diplomacy,' the newly combative style of diplomacy adopted under Xi Jinping and named after a jingoistic series of Chinese action films.[36] Needless to say, this represents a fundamental, inescapable challenge to the American-led Westphalian order, making strife of some kind unavoidable.[37]

2.2 The Cerberean Method

The CCP's geopolitical *modus operandi* is perhaps best described as Cerberean, after the hound of Hades: a tripartite policy of extraction, projection, and subversion protruding from the singular beast of Sinocentric *Weltpolitik*.[38] Each head shall be discussed in turn.

---

31 Kissinger, *On China*, 23.
32 See Kissinger, *World Order*, 226–232. For a historical account of China's impressive long-term progress in this regard, see Orville Schell and John Delury, *Wealth and Power: China's Long March to the Twentieth Century* (London: Abacus, 2013).
33 Simon Schama, *Citizens: A Chronicle of the French Revolution* (Knopf, 1989), 860. See Frank Dikotter's superlative trilogy: *The Tragedy of Liberation* (Bloomsbury, 2013), *Mao's Great Famine* (Bloomsbury, 2010) and *The Cultural Revolution* (Bloomsbury, 2016).
34 Frank Dikotter, *China after Mao: The Rise of a Superpower* (Bloomsbury, 2022).
35 Perry Link, "China: The Anaconda in the Chandelier," *ChinaFile*, April 11, 2002, https://www.chinafile.com/library/nyrb-china-archive/china-anaconda-chandelier.
36 Peter Martin, *China's Civilian Army: The Making of Wolf Warrior Diplomacy* (Oxford: Oxford University Press, 2021), 2–5.
37 White, "Reordering the Law for a China World Order," 442–443.
38 This is, of course, consistent with their global ambitions, ideology, and methods – see generally Clive Hamilton and Mareike Ohlberg, *Hidden Hand: Exposing how the Chinese Communist Party is Reshaping the World* (London: Oneworld, 2020).

2.2.1 Extractive Techniques

Communist regimes are typically as poor at innovation as they are adept at extracting what they need from hapless Western institutions. The potential for scientific research to unsettle rigid ideological beliefs was well-understood by the Soviets who politicized research to such a degree that it hampered originality and, despite lavish state funding, forced them to parasitize foreign breakthroughs.[39] By the 1980s, for example, at least 70% of all Warsaw Pact weapons systems were based on stolen Western technology acquired primarily from infiltrated American businesses and British universities, while the Cambridge Five supplied such a 'volume of high-grade intelligence ... that Moscow sometimes had difficulty coping with it.'[40] As with the Soviets during the Cold War, so with the CCP since Deng Xiaoping's 'four modernizations' drive of 1978 enabled China to exploit global neoliberalism and imbue it with 'Chinese characteristics.'[41] As recently as 2019, Xi Jinping acknowledged China's 'lack of strength in innovation ability, which is the "Achilles heel" of this lug of an economy of ours.'[42] To offset this disadvantage, the CCP has long employed illicit and legal means to acquire strategic intellectual property and technology.

The threat from traditional 'secret' espionage began to escalate during the 1980s although Western counterintelligence could not 'pretend to anything like satisfactory coverage,' and Western firms remained lax about 'the weight and intensity of the Chinese Intelligence effort.'[43] Over the past decade, the threat has intensified again: 69% of the 224 publicly reported instances of Chinese espionage directed at the United States from 2000 to March 2023 occurred after Xi Jinping took senior office in 2012, while the vast majority of the 147 China-related indictments or convictions of individuals for economic espionage or trade secret theft since 2004 occurred between 2010 and 2019.[44] Using Signals Intelligence (SIGINT) from well-resourced cyberwarfare operations and Human Intelligence (HUMINT) from large Chinese diasporas and

---

39 See generally Simon Ings, *Stalin and the Scientists: A History of the Triumph and Tragedy 1905–1953* (London: Faber & Faber, 2017).

40 Christopher Andrew and Vasili Mitrokhin, *The Mitrokhin Archive Vol I: The KGB in Europe and the West* (London: Penguin, 2018), 75–76, 549, 597, 724.

41 David Harvey, *A Brief History of Neoliberalism* (Oxford: Oxford University Press, 2007), 120.

42 See, "Lack of innovation is 'Achilles heel' for China's economy, Xi says," *Reuters*, May 16, 2019, https://www.reuters.com/article/us-china-politics-xi-idUSKCN1SM08G; and William C. Hannas and Huey-Meei Chang, "Chinese technology transfer – an introduction," in William C. Hannas and Didi Kristen Tatlow, eds., *China's Quest for Foreign Technology: Beyond Espionage* (New York: Routledge, 2021), 7–8.

43 Christopher Andrew, *The Defence of the Realm: The Authorised History of MI5* (London: Penguin, 2010), 731.

44 "Survey of Chinese Espionage in the United States Since 2000," *Centre for Strategic & International Studies*, accessed December 31, 2023, https://www.csis.org/programs/strategic-technologies-program/survey-chinese-espionage-united-states-2000; and James Mulvenon, "Economic espionage and trade secret theft cases in the US," in Hannas and Tatlow, *China's Quest for Foreign Technology,* 295–296.

student populations, for decades the CCP has been pirating items on its 'modernization shopping list' in every field from biological warfare via information technology through advanced robotics to nuclear weaponry.[45] Perhaps the most remarkable heist occurred between 1964 and 1983, during which time a French diplomat handed over 100 classified documents to his lover, Shi Pei Pu, a purportedly female opera diva who – despite their 20-year affair – turned out to be a 'modest' male agent and the inspiration behind the subsequent Broadway hit, *M(onsieur) Butterfly*.[46] More recently, during a UK Prime Ministerial trade delegation to Shanghai in 2008, one of Gordon Brown's senior advisors gleefully bedded a honeypot and woke up 'minus his Blackberry and half the contents of his suitcase.'[47]

A recent FBI report estimated that Chinese technology theft, which costs around '$300 billion–$600 billion a year,' represents the greatest law enforcement threat to the US, with multiple arrests annually and '1,000 investigations involving China's attempted theft of US-based technology in all 56 of our field offices and spanning just about every industry sector.'[48] However, Western analysts are prone to imposing their own cultural assumptions on Chinese espionage in a mistaken attempt to make it 'conform to a world it does not inhabit.'[49]

Surgical intelligence gathering is not the only or even the most important means by which China acquires strategic assets and information. As neither the Chinese language nor the CCP distinguish between 'intelligence' and 'information,' China's espionage apparatus – now the largest in the world – is unlike anything in the West.[50] While the Ministry of State Security (MSS) is

45 Roger Faligot, *Chinese Spies from Chairman Mao to Xi Jinping* (London: Hurst, 2019), 251, 334.
46 Andrew and Green, *Stars and Spies*, 340–341.
47 Richard J. Aldrich and Rory Cormac, *The Black Door: Spies, Secret Intelligence and British Prime Ministers* (London: William Collins, 2017), 454; see also Phillip Knightly, "The History of the Honey Trap," *Foreign Policy*, March 12, 2010, https://foreignpolicy.com/2010/03/12/the -history-of-the-honey-trap.
48 "China theft of technology is biggest law enforcement threat to US, FBI says," *The Guardian*, February 6, 2020, https://www.theguardian.com/world/2020/feb/06/china-technology -theft-fbi-biggest-threat; and Dave Lee, "Chinese man pleads guilty to US military hack," *BBC News*, March 23, 2016, https://www.bbc.co.uk/news/technology-35888106; "Former State Department Employee Sentenced for Conspiring with Chinese Agents," *US Department of Justice*, July 9, 2019, https://www.justice.gov/opa/pr/former-state-department-employee -sentenced-conspiring-chinese-agents; and Faligot, *Chinese Spies from Chairman Mao to Xi Jinping*, 421–423.
49 Gordon Corera, *Intercept: The Secret History of Computers and Spies from Bletchley Park to Cyber Espionage* (London: W&N, 2016), 183.
50 I.C. Smith and Nigel West, *Historical Dictionary of Chinese Intelligence*, 2nd ed. (Lanham, Md.: Rowman & Littlefield, 2021), 220; and Faligot, *Chinese Spies from Chairman Mao to Xi Jinping*, 401.

the closest counterpart to the CIA or MI6, and various other state and People's Liberation Army (PLA) organs have carved out parallel niches, there is no meaningful separation between military and civilian, domestic and foreign, or professional and amateur when it comes to intelligence collection.[51] This is the 'thousand grains of sand approach' whereby the CCP processes 'mammoth' quantities of data procured by any means from every available source: specialist spies, state-sponsored hackers, devices within Chinese-manufactured components of government cars, open-source online resources, diplomats, journalists, tourists, businessmen, STEM students, expatriates, Western traitors, unscrupulous RAF pilots and hapless MoD training schemes, poached foreign academics, partnerships with Western universities, multinational corporations sharing trade secrets for access to the Chinese market, takeovers of Western companies by state-backed enterprises – the list is potentially endless.[52]

In practice, this means that most of the intelligence and technology China receives about and from the West is probably obtained lawfully; indeed, the CCP openly promotes its acquisitive intentions and technology transfer programs.[53] To give a sense of scale, there have been 1,200 cases of intellectual property theft litigation brought by American companies against Chinese entities since 2000 in either the US or Chinese jurisdictions, with 'thousands' more complaints brought and investigations opened into non-traditional espionage activity; a recent DOJ report estimated that China was behind 90% of all (traditional and non-traditional) economic espionage cases between 2011 and 2018; the Office of the United States Trade Representative (USTR) has released successive special reports reiterating significant concerns with intellectual property safety in China (Priority Watch List); and the FBI's assistant director of counter-intelligence recently observed that 'Every rock we turn over, every time we look for it, it is not only there – it is worse than anticipated.'[54]

51 Peter Mattis, "Beyond Spy vs. Spy: The Analytic Challenge of Understanding Chinese Intelligence Services," *Studies in Intelligence*, Vol. 56, No. 3 (September 2012), 52; and Faligot, *Chinese Spies from Chairman Mao to Xi Jinping*, 402–403.
52 Corera, *Intercept*, 184–186; Hamilton and Ohlberg, *Hidden Hand*, 140–141; Smith and West, *Historical Dictionary of Chinese Intelligence*, 401; Deborah Haynes, "UK sent RAF pilots to teach Chinese counterparts and allowed students to attend British military colleges," *Sky News*, October 28, 2022; Madeleine Ross, "Chinese tracking device is 'discovered inside UK government car,' as senior politician slams Beijing as a 'systematic' threat to Britain's security," *Daily Mail*, January 6, 2023, https://www.dailymail.co.uk/news/article-11607735/Chinese-tracking-device-discovered-inside-UK-government-car-senior-politician-slams-Beijing.html.
53 Hannas and Chang, "Chinese technology transfer – an introduction," in Hannas and Tatlow, *China's Quest for Foreign Technology*, 6–12.
54 "Survey of Chinese Espionage in the United States Since 2000"; "2022 Special 301 Report," (Office of the United States Trade Representative (USTR), April 2022), 44–53 and "2023 Spe-

Such are the fruits of the CCP's bid to overcome China's 'indigenous creativity problem' with a 'composite innovation system' to supercharge economic growth.[55] Innovation Chinese-style, in other words, consists of repurposing and refining foreign inventions in accordance with CCP priorities before commercializing much of it at scale for a domestic market with the assistance of highly advanced fintech.[56] This 'sea lamprey strategy' 'has merit' enough to 'be confronted on its own terms as a viable developmental model,' even though 'there is little prospect it will transition to a 'normal' (Western) model on its own.'[57] Indeed, the results speak for themselves: China's economy is now the world's second largest, and that means the CCP can leverage its growing financial might to project power like never before.[58]

2.2.2 *Projective Techniques*

As is characteristic of the communist regimes it spawned, Soviet Russia was an expansionary power. Its militarism is attested to from the earliest attempts to overrun Poland and topple British India using jihadist proxies, through the subsequent creation of a system of overseas bases throughout Eastern Europe, the Middle East, Asia, and Africa, to the final, fatal bid to entrench a pliant regime in Afghanistan.[59] The Soviets were also adept at employing more subtle means to project soft power into their strongest adversaries, notably by establishing the Communist International (Comintern) and its successor organizations to wage psychological warfare, spread propaganda, and coordinate front groups throughout the West.[60] For example, between 1919 and 1922,

cial 301 Report," (Office of the United States Trade Representative (USTR), April 2023), 45–55; Hamilton and Ohlberg, *Hidden Hand*, 140.
55 Hannas and Chang, "Chinese technology transfer – an introduction," in Hannas and Tatlow, *China's Quest for Foreign* Technology, 3.
56 Elizabeth C. Economy, *The Third Revolution: Xi Jinping and the New Chinese State* (Oxford: Oxford University Press, 2019), 124–126.
57 Faligot, *Chinese Spies from Chairman Mao to Xi Jinping*, 282–285; Hannas and Chang, "Chinese technology transfer – an introduction," in Hannas and Tatlow, *China's Quest for Foreign* Technology, 3.
58 "GDP by Country," *Worldometer*, accessed October 23, 2023, https://www.worldometers.info/gdp/gdp-by-country.
59 See generally and respectively: Adam Zamoyski, *Warsaw 1920: Lenin's Failed Conquest of Europe* (London: William Collins, 2014); Giles Milton, *Russian Roulette: How British Spies Defeated Lenin* (London: John Murray, 2014), Robert E. Harkavy, *Bases Abroad: The Global Foreign Military Presence* (Oxford: Oxford University Press, 1989); and Roderic Braithwaite, *Afgantsy: The Russians in Afghanistan 1979–89* (Profile, 2012).
60 Nicholas J. Cull, "Reading, Viewing, and Tuning in to the Cold War," in Melvyn Leffler and Odd Arne Westad, eds., *The Cambridge History of the Cold War, Volume II: Crises and Détente* (Cambridge University Press, 2010), 439; and Bernard S. Morris, "Communist International Front Organisations: Their Nature and Functions," *World Politics*, Vol. 9, No. 1 (1956), 76–87.

the Comintern acquired 440,000 international members and 61 affiliated parties.[61] The Communist Party of the United States of America was underwritten by gold and diamonds smuggled in from Moscow via a chain of middlemen, while the Communist Party of Great Britain also received policy directives and 'substantial' secret subsidies from the Comintern.[62] Throughout the Cold War, Moscow maintained and infiltrated a staggering array of Western organizations – trade unions, student societies, 'peace' movements, international NGOs, UN bodies, *ad infinitum* – for the purposes of harvesting intelligence, undermining enemies, and amplifying influence.[63]

While Western powers sometimes responded in ways that 'came close to undermining the very way of life that was being protected,' the CCP began to forge its own global network of pro-Chinese fronts, and there are striking parallels between the *modus operandi* of the Soviets and contemporary PRC.[64] In terms of hard power, China's military expenditure (anywhere between $225 and $700 billion annually) now ranks second in the world and is greater than that of at least the next three top powers combined.[65] Aside from increasing and improving its conventional capabilities, China is also investing in overseas bases such as the Chinese People's Liberation Army Support Base in Djibouti (constructed in 2016) while purchasing or constructing strategic infrastructure (ranging from ports to telecommunications to mining facilities) across Europe, Asia, and Africa.[66]

The projection of Chinese soft power falls within Beijing's 'United Front strategy' which is regarded by Party theorists as the science of 'forging the broadest possible coalition of interests so as to undermine the "chief enemy"' (i.e. the West).[67] Alongside Party building and armed struggle, Xi Jinping (following Mao) recently described United Front work as 'an important magic weapon for strengthening the party's ruling position and for realising

61 Wilfred Loth, "The Cold War and social and economic history," in Melvyn Leffler and Odd Arne Westad, *The Cambridge History of the Cold War, Volume II: Crises and Détente*, 505.
62 Tim Weiner, *Enemies: A History of the FBI* (London: Penguin, 2013), 27; Andrew, *The Defence of the Realm*, 135, 148.
63 See generally Robert Service, *Comrades! Communism: A World History* (London: Pan, 2008).
64 Anne Deighton, "Britain and the Cold War 1945–55," in Melvyn Leffler and Odd Arne Westad, *The Cambridge History of the Cold War, Volume I: Origins* (Cambridge: Cambridge University Press, 2010), 124; Michael D. Gambone, *Capturing the Revolution: The United States, Central America and Nicaragua 1961–72* (Westport, Conn.: Praeger, 2001), 129; and Alaba Ogunsanwo, *China's Policy in Africa 1958–71* (Cambridge: Cambridge University Press, 1974), 96–97.
65 China Power, "What Does China Really Spend on its Military?," *Center for Strategic and International Studies (CSIS)*, November 9, 2023, https://chinapower.csis.org/military-spending/; Peter Robertson and Wilson Beaver, "China's Defense Budget Is Much Bigger Than It Looks," *Foreign Policy*, September 9, 2023, https://foreignpolicy.com/2023/09/19/china-defense-budget -military-weapons-purchasing-power/.
66 See generally Bruno Macaes, *Belt and Road: A Chinese World Order* (London: Hurst, 2020).
67 Anne-Marie Brady quoted in Hamilton and Ohlberg, *Hidden Hand*, 16–17.

the China Dream of the Great Rejuvenation of the Chinese Nation.'[68] Such work is the responsibility of every Party member as well as the United Front, a globe-spanning network 'formally tasked with building support for the CCP and neutralizing its political enemies.'[69] With a budget larger than that of the entire Ministry of Foreign Affairs, which it outranks, the United Front is overseen jointly by two organs of the CCP: the United Front Work Department (UFWD) and the Chinese People's Political Consultative Conference (CPPCC).[70]

United Front activity in the West is chiefly about 'repurposing democratic governance structures to serve as tools of extraterritorial influence.'[71] One of its 'public faces' in the West is the Chinese People's Association for Friendship with Foreign Countries (CPAFFC), which manages China's sister city relationships to secure 'all round influence' over everything from orchestras to panda deliveries.[72] Typically clandestine, however, the United Front's work involves dominating Chinese diasporas, co-opting foreign supporters, pushing CCP propaganda, advancing China's economic interests, and gathering intelligence, all while maintaining plausible deniability.[73] While some organizations belong to the United Front proper, others may/do not and simply conduct themselves as useful/venal idiots in ways or towards ends that benefit the CCP.[74]

The United Front strategy encompasses both sorts of entity and is directed in particular at political, business, and intellectual elites.[75] The foundation in 1954 of the London-based 48 Group Club, for example, 'was the work of three secret members of the Communist Party of Great Britain' ostensibly to

68 Quoted in Alex Joske, *The party speaks for you: foreign interference and the Chinese Communist Party's United Front system* (Australian Strategic Policy Institute, June 2020), 4, https://www.aspi.org.au/report/party-speaks-you; and Anne-Marie Brady, *Magic Weapons: China's political influence activities under Xi Jinping* (Washington D. C.: Wilson Center, September 18, 2017), 7, https://www.wilsoncenter.org/sites/default/files/media/documents/article/magic_weapons.pdf.

69 Hamilton and Ohlberg, *Hidden Hand*, 17; and Hayton, *The Invention of China*, 76.

70 Richard McGregor, *The Party: The Secret World of China's Communist Rulers* (London: Penguin, 2012), 16–17; and Didi Kirsten Tatlow, "Exclusive: 600 U.S. Groups Linked to Chinese Communist Party Influence Effort with Ambition Beyond Election," *Newsweek*, October 26, 2020, https://www.newsweek.com/2020/11/13/exclusive-600-us-groups-linked-chinese-communist-party-influence-effort-ambition-beyond-1541624.html.

71 Jichang Lulu, "Repurposing Democracy: The European Parliament China Friendship Cluster," *Sinopsis*, November 26, 2019, https://sinopsis.cz/wp-content/uploads/2019/11/ep.pdf, 1.

72 Larry Diamond and Orville Schell, *China's Influence and American Interests: Promoting Constructive Vigilance* (Washington D. C.: Hoover Institution Press, 2019), 187; and Nick Cohen, "China's obsessive attempts to subvert the West," *The Spectator*, September 21, 2021.

73 Anne-Marie Brady, "New Zealand: Anne-Marie Brady's parliamentary submission on political interference," *Sinopsis*, May 10, 2019, https://sinopsis.cz/en/new-zealand-anne-marie-bradys-parliamentary-submission-on-political-interference.

74 Following the convention set by Hamilton and Ohlberg, *Hidden Hand*, 16.

75 Ibid., 16–18.

promote 'Equality and Mutual Benefit' through UK–China trade.[76] However, the Group and its Chairman, Stephen Perry, actively promote China's Belt and Road Initiative, reproduce CCP narratives, and enjoy unrivalled access to Xi Jinping himself – 'no group in Britain enjoys more intimacy and trust with the CCP leadership.'[77] In 2020, Perry launched an unsuccessful libel action in the English courts to prevent the publication of an academic exposé, *Hidden Hand: Exposing How the CCP is Reshaping the World*; asked whether he believed the CCP was behind the move, one of the authors, Professor Clive Hamilton, said: 'I have no evidence of that, although it should be noted that the Chinese government has used lawfare in the past.'[78] Three publishers rejected Hamilton's previous study of CCP influence in Australia out of fear of legal 'retaliation' from Chinese entities.[79] Regardless, the 48 Group Club has over 500 high-society members including Tony Blair, Peter Mandelson, Michael Heseltine, Alex Salmond, and Professor Peter Nolan of Jesus College at the University of Cambridge.[80] Nolan and Jesus College have themselves been implicated in China-related controversy: the former for appearing to caution students against harming 'mutual understanding' with China by raising the treatment of Uyghur Muslims in debates, and the latter for accepting large sums from Chinese entities to fund professorships, sensitive research, and a China Centre.[81]

The proliferation of Chinese Students and Scholars Associations – for 'non-political social and cultural activities among Chinese students and scholars' – and Confucius Institutes – for promoting 'Chinese language and culture' – has generated concerns over espionage, interference with academic freedom and freedom of expression, failing professional and institutional integrity, and harassment or intimidation campaigns against dissident students

---

76 Ibid., 64; Martin Purbrick, "United Front Work and Beyond: How the Chinese Communist Party Penetrates the United States and Western Societies," *The Jamestown Foundation*, April 12, 2023, https://jamestown.org/program/united-front-work-and-beyond-how-the-chinese-communist-party-penetrates-the-united-states-and-western-societies/.

77 Ibid., 60–62; and Zhang Yunbi, "Xi hails legacy, key role of UK 'icebreakers,'" *China Daily*, July 7, 2023, https://www.chinadaily.com.cn/a/202307/07/WS64a6e16ca310bf8a75d6dacf.html.

78 Robert Fife and Steven Chase, "Legal challenge halts Canadian, U.S. and U.K. release of book critical of Chinese Communist Party," *The Globe and Mail*, June 19, 2020, https://www.theglobeandmail.com/politics/article-legal-challenge-halts-canadian-us-and-uk-release-of-book-critical.

79 "Controversial China 'influence' book to be published," *BBC News*, February 6, 2018, https://www.bbc.co.uk/news/world-australia-42954476.

80 Hamilton and Ohlberg, *Hidden Hand*, 60–64.

81 Lauren Lewis, "Cambridge don, 72, cautioned students against debating Uighur Muslims because it would damage 'mutual understanding' with China and instead appear like a 'campaign for freedom in Hong Kong,'" *MailOnline*, June 6, 2021, https://www.dailymail.co.uk/news/article-9657325/Cambridge-don-72-told-students-not-debate-Uighur-Muslims.html; and Lucy Fisher, "Jesus college accepted £155,000 contribution from Huawei," *The Times*, July 10, 2020, https://www.thetimes.co.uk/article/jesus-college-accepted-155-000-contribution-from-huawei-53rr7qmcf.

and academics.[82] This network was openly described by the CCP's former propaganda chief as 'an important part of China's overseas propaganda set-up.'[83] There are countless other examples from countless other sectors of the United Front strategy at work – think-tanks courted and created, independent schools acquired, pubs visited by Xi Jinping bought up, celebrities pressured into obsequiousness – but as a general rule the CCP will encourage, establish, or invest in any institution with practical or prestige value.[84]

The penetration and prostration of Western elites is nothing, however, compared to what is occurring in developing regions such as Pakistan where the CCP has created a dependency so overwhelming that the two nations have formed a de facto military axis against the US and India.[85] This presents a particular danger to the UK where (1) the 'policy-making process ([and] "establishment") with respect to Pakistan is strongly influenced by a skilful and far-reaching Pakistani lobby' and which (2) launched the 'PAK-UK Education Gateway' (PUKEG) to facilitate Pakistan's access to high-tech education and sensitive technology including 'artificial intelligence, robotics, nanotechnology big data and cloud computing... to name a few.'[86] Given Pakistan's history of technology theft via the A.Q. Khan network, and that the China–Pakistan Economic Corridor (CPEC, Belt and Road) involves large-scale research collaboration via a 'Consortium of Universities' and the 'China-Pakistan Higher Education Research Institute,' the UK's historic ties with Pakistan leave it highly vulnerable to China's mendicant 'all-weather friend.'[87] In this way, then, the CCP

---

82 Hamilton and Ohlberg, *Hidden Hand*, 226–248.

83 Ibid., 228.

84 Ibid.; Jake Ryan, Glen Owen, and Jonathan Bucks, "The British schools selling out to Beijing: Not only are private institutions being bought by Chinese firms but some are giving communist-approved lessons that are a threat to free speech," *MailOnline*, February 21, 2021, https://www.dailymail.co.uk/news/article-9282617/British-private-institutions-bought-Chinese-firms.html; Vincent Ni, "John Cena 'very sorry' for saying Taiwan is a country," *The Guardian*, May 25, 2021, https://www.theguardian.com/world/2021/may/26/john-cena-very-sorry-for-saying-taiwan-is-a-country; and David Cameron, *For the Record* (London: William Collins, 2020), 620.

85 For country-specific examples see Clive Hamilton, *Silent Invasion: China's influence in Australia* (Melbourne: Hardie Grant, 2018), John Manthorpe, *Claws of the Panda: Beijing's Campaign of Influence and Intimidation in Canada* (Toronto: Cormorant, 2019); and Andrew Small, *The China-Pakistan Axis: Asia's New Geopolitics* (London: Hurst, 2020).

86 Shaun Gregory, "Written Evidence on The UK's Foreign Policy towards Afghanistan and Pakistan" (Foreign Affairs Select Committee, October 18, 2010), https://publications.parliament.uk/pa/cm201011/cmselect/cmfaff/writev/afpak/afpak15.htm; British Council Pakistan, "Pak-UK Education Gateway: Innovative, Impactful and Collaborative Research" (British Council, December 2020), https://www.britishcouncil.pk/programmes/education/higher-education/pak-uk-education-gateway.

87 See Michael Laufer, "A. Q. Khan Nuclear Chronology" (Carnegie Endowment for International Peace, September 7, 2005), https://carnegieendowment.org/2005/09/07/a.-q.-khan-nuclear-chronology-pub-17420; Zahid Anwar, "Exploring Academic Collaboration with Chinese Universities under CPEC" (University of Peshawar China Study Center, January 31, 2021), https://cscp.edu.pk/2021/01/31/exploring-academic-collaboration-with-chinese-universities-under

cultivates proxies with the means and motive to acquire sensitive technology from the 'chief enemy,' all while undermining Western alliances and sapping their resistance as part of a concerted campaign of subversion.

2.2.3 Subversive Techniques

Without exception, communist regimes attain and retain power through subversion.[88] The Soviets were, as usual, pioneering in their methods. Soon after the 1917 Revolution, for example, Lenin hollowed out every domestic institution capable of catalyzing opposition – from churches to schools to clubs – by turning them into compliant 'Potemkin Institutions' subservient to Party ideology rather than the purposes of their members.[89] Later in the Cold War, the USSR attempted to subvert Western economic strength by restricting access to strategic resources such as gold and diamonds and keeping market prices high. While this did not ultimately have the desired impact on its enemies, Moscow did covertly establish 'something approaching a duopoly' on precious minerals with apartheid South Africa, all while denouncing Western competitors for doing business with a racist regime.[90] Nevertheless, the Soviets were remarkably successful at subverting British intelligence, industry, and media.[91] Familiar tactics included: interfering with elections, spreading disinformation to harass and discredit prominent critics, planting fake news in the mainstream media, using activists to inflame political tensions, infiltrating and corrupting Western institutions, forging diplomatic documents to undermine alliances, inciting unrest or rebellions to destabilize hostile nations, funding proxies for all manner of purposes, goading enemies into humiliating overreactions – the list goes on.[92] These 'active measures' were really 'munitions of

---

-cpec/; Faseeh Mangi, "China's Funding to Pakistan Stands at 30% of Foreign Debt" (Bloomberg, September 2, 2022), https://www.bloomberg.com/news/articles/2022-09-02/china-s-funding-to-pakistan-stands-at-30-of-foreign-debt; Small, *The China-Pakistan Axis*, blurb.

88 See generally Archie Brown, *The Rise and Fall of Communism* (New York: Vintage, 2010).

89 Roger Scruton and John Finnis, "Corporate Persons," *Proceedings of the Aristotelian Society, Supplementary Volumes*, Vol. 63 (1989), 262.

90 Christopher Andrew and Vasili Mitrokhin, *The Mitrokhin Archive Vol II: The KGB in the World* (London: Penguin, 2018), 468–469.

91 See Ben Macintyre, *A Spy Among Friends: Philby and the Great Betrayal* (London: Bloomsbury, 2015); Andrew, *The Defence of the Realm*, 406–411; and Andrew and Mitrokhin, *The Mitrokhin Archive Vol II*, 557.

92 See generally Nicholas J. Cull, Vasily Gatov, Peter Pomerantsev, Anne Applebaum, and Alistair Shawcross, "Soviet Subversion, Disinformation and Propaganda: How the West Fought Against it – An Analytic History, with Lessons for the Present – Final Report" (London: LSE Consulting, October 2017), https://www.lse.ac.uk/business/consulting/reports/soviet-subversion-disinformation-and-propaganda-how-the-west-fought-against-it.

the mind' designed to encourage fanatics, persuade the gullible, and corrode the cohesion and trust that held Western societies together.[93]

Anything the Soviets did the CCP can now do better and at scale.[94] While the Cultural Revolution was perhaps the greatest act of civilizational subversion in history, the CCP routinely subverts the remaining pillars of Chinese civil society.[95] For example, China's infamous one-child policy (now a three-child policy) was intended to control population growth and family composition and has officially been responsible for preventing 400 million births between 1979 and 2016; many of the enforcement methods developed during that period – from forcible sterilization and compulsory abortions – have since been used to reduce the Muslim Uyghur population in Xinjiang province.[96] In 2018, the CCP obtained a 'non-political provisional agreement' from the Vatican which promised to encourage the laity to register with the Chinese Catholic Patriotic Association (CCPA) and allow the CCP to approve bishops before their appointment by the pope. As of 2020, the CCP was already reneging on the terms of the agreement and set about arresting dissident nuns in Hong Kong.[97] Further, the CCP has constructed a 'Great Firewall of China' to filter out sensitive online information for domestic consumers – UK universities offering distance learning have been only too happy to comply[98] – and has even sought to restrict the use of video games, prevent the promotion of 'sissy' entertainers, and ban karaoke songs with 'illegal content.'[99] In short,

93 Philip M. Taylor, *Munitions of the Mind: A History of Propaganda from the Ancient World to the Present Day*, 3rd ed. (Manchester, U.K.: Manchester University Press, 2003), 266.

94 And has been doing since its inception: see "China's Methods of Subversion: Journals to subvert the minds; Journalists to subvert the regimes," *China Report*, Vol. 2, No.1 (1966), 20–22.

95 See Frank Dikotter, *The Cultural Revolution: A People's History 1962–1976* (Bloomsbury, 2016).

96 Justin Parkinson, "Who are the Uyghurs and why is China being accused of genocide?" *BBC News*, June 21, 2021, https://www.bbc.co.uk/news/world-asia-china-22278037; "China allows three children in major policy shift," *BBC News*, May 31, 2021, https://www.bbc.co.uk/news/world-asia-china-57303592; "China cuts Uighur births with IUDs, abortion, sterilization," *The Associated Press*, June 29, 2020 https://apnews.com/article/ap-top-news-international-news-weekend-reads-china-health-269b3de1af34e17c1941a514f78d764c.

97 Rogers, "China Is Already Breaking Its Vatican Deal."; Michael Sainsbury, "China and Catholicism, an unhappy Marriage," *The Lowy Institute*, October 14, 2019, https://www.lowyinstitute.org/the-interpreter/china-and-catholicism-unhappy-marriage; and Greg Torode, "Nuns arrested as Beijing turns up heat on Church in Hong Kong," *Reuters*, December 30, 2020, https://www.reuters.com/investigates/special-report/hongkong-security-church.

98 Sean Coughlan, "UK universities comply with China's internet restrictions," *BBC News*, July 9, 2020, https://www.bbc.com/news/education-53341217.

99 Elizabeth Economy, "The great firewall of China: Xi Jinping's internet shutdown," *The Guardian*, June 29, 2018, https://www.theguardian.com/news/2018/jun/29/the-great-firewall-of-china-xi-jinpings-internet-shutdown; "China bans under-18s from playing online games for more than an hour a day," *Sky News*, August 30, 2021, https://news.sky.com/story/china-bans-under-18s-from-playing-online-games-for-more-than-an-hour-a-day-12395135; Vincent Ni, "China bans reality talent shows to curb behaviours of 'idol' fandoms," *The Guardian*, September 2,

the Party is extending its control into the most intimate areas of life to subvert any institution, artifact, or practice that could catalyze domestic opposition. Foreign adversaries are dealt with in much the same way.

Whereas the Nixon administration was once able to exacerbate and exploit the Sino-Soviet split through rapprochement with Mao, today it is the CCP that is busily sowing division among Western powers.[100] New Zealand under former Prime Minister Jacinda Ardern has proved itself 'the weak link' in the Five Eyes intelligence alliance (also including the US, UK, Canada, and Australia) now that China has become its largest trading partner.[101] In 2021, Ardern's Labour administration urged Australia, which had been hit with Chinese trade sanctions, to 'follow us and show respect, I guess a little more diplomacy from time to time, and be cautious' and later announced that New Zealand would henceforth 'maintain and respect' China's 'particular customs, traditions and values' and not allow the Five Eyes to determine national foreign policy.[102] The CCP's success in this regard was a result of making New Zealand overly reliant upon their bilateral economic relationship, leveraging the effects of its trade war against Australia as a warning to the smaller nation and exploiting New Zealand's tardiness in adjusting 'to China's aggressive international strategy.'[103]

China has adopted similar tactics against other US allies including Israel, Lithuania, and the European Union as part of a broader campaign against the US-led 'rules-based international order.'[104] At the same time, it 'is in the

---

2021, https://www.theguardian.com/world/2021/sep/02/china-bans-reality-talent-shows-to-curb -behaviours-of-idol-fandoms; and "China to ban karaoke songs with 'illegal content' that endangers national unity," *The Guardian*, August 11, 2019, https://www.theguardian.com/world/2021/ aug/11/china-to-ban-karaoke-songs-with-content-that-endangers-national-unity.

100 See Jonathan Fenby, *The Penguin History of Modern China: The Fall and Rise of a Great Power 1850 to the Present*, 3rd ed. (London: Penguin, 2019), 499–507.

101 "New Zealand's Stance on China Has Deep Implications for the Five Eyes Alliance," *The Guardian*, April 23, 2021, https://www.theguardian.com/world/2021/apr/23/new-zealands -stance-on-china-has-deep-implications-for-the-five-eyes-alliance.

102 "New Zealand Trade Minister Tries to Ease Tensions after Saying Australia Should 'Show Respect' to China," *The Guardian*, January 28, 2021, https://www.theguardian.com/australia -news/2021/jan/28/china-calls-on-australia-to-follow-new-zealands-lead-in-how-it-deals-with -beijing; and Steerpike, "Has the Shine Come off Saint Jacinda?" *The Spectator*, April 20, 2021, https://www.spectator.co.uk/article/is-the-shine-coming-off-saint-jacinda-.

103 William Stoltz, "Five Eyes Split Demands Australia Reset with New Zealand," *The Sydney Morning Herald*, April 25, 2021, https://www.smh.com.au/national/five-eyes-split-demands -australia-reset-with-new-zealand-20210423-p57lsw.html.

104 Jake Wallis Simons, "How China Drove a Wedge between America and Israel," *The Spectator*, August 30, 2021, https://www.spectator.co.uk/article/how-china-drove-a-wedge-between -america-and-israel; Helen Davidson, "China's Trade Halt with Lithuania over Taiwan Ties Sends Warning to Europe," *The Guardian*, August 26, 2021, https://www.theguardian.com/ world/2021/aug/26/chinas-trade-halt-with-lithuania-over-taiwan-ties-sends-warning-to -europe; and Thorsten Benner, Jan Gaspers, Mareike Ohlberg, Lucrezia Poggetti, and Kristin Shi-Kupfer, "Authoritarian Advance: Responding to China's Growing Political Influence in

process of dominating the export and consumption of rare metals' used to make Western weapons systems and most electronic technologies.[105] China mines between 70% and 90% of the planet's rare earth minerals and owns 36.7% of global totals, against the US's 12.2% and 1.1% respective share of production and ownership.[106] While its export quotas, duties, and restrictions on these resources were successfully challenged in 2014 through international litigation before the World Trade Organization, the West remains at a considerable geopolitical disadvantage for as long as China remains the 'Rare Metals Master.'[107] This threat was brought into sharp relief in 2022 when the Pentagon suspended deliveries of F-35 jets from Lockheed Martin after Chinese magnetic alloys were discovered in all 600 planes hitherto delivered, before quickly granting the manufacturer a special waiver on national security grounds out of sheer necessity.[108] Alliances and access to strategic resources are not the only targets of Chinese subversion, however; the CCP is also attacking the very fabric of social cohesion that holds Western democracies together.

Unlike the Soviets, who generally struggled to interpret political intelligence, the CCP has perceptively seized upon Western culture wars to create mischief and delegitimize US initiatives.[109] There is ample evidence for this, not least in the existence of the specific Chinese word, *Baizuo*, for the self-hating 'white left who only care about topics such as immigration, minorities, LGBT and the environment... to satisfy their own feelings of moral superiority', and its gendered variant, *Shengmubiao,* which translates as 'holy mother bitch' and denotes those who are so 'woke' that they have emasculated themselves by obsessing over 'the silly, overly sentimental issues soft-hearted women care about.'[110] Moreover, the CCP possesses a vast array of institutions

Europe," *GPPi & MERICS*, February 5, 2018, https://www.gppi.net/2018/02/05/authoritarian-advance-responding-to-chinas-growing-political-influence-in-europe.

105 Guillaume Pitron, *The Rare Metals War: The Dark Side of Clean Energy and Digital Technologies* (Melbourne: Scribe, 2020), 3–4, 9.

106 Kittrie, *Lawfare*, 188–189; and Ariel Cohen and James C. Grant, "America's Critical Strategic Vulnerability: Rare Earth Elements," *Foreign Policy Research Institute*, June 22, 2021, https://www.fpri.org/article/2021/06/americas-critical-strategic-vulnerability-rare-earth-elements.

107 Kittrie, *Lawfare*, 188–189; and Hubert Vedrine, quoted in Pitron, *The Rare Metals War: The Dark Side of Clean Energy and Digital Technologies*, x.

108 Lara Seligman, "China Dominates the Rare Earths Market. This U.S. Mine Is Trying to Change That," Politico, December 14, 2022, https://www.politico.com/news/magazine/2022/12/14/rare-earth-mines-00071102.

109 Andrew and Mitrokhin, *The Mitrokhin Archive, Vol I*, 723; and John Hudson, "Biden administration begins first faceoff with China amid worsening relations," *Washington Post*, March 18, 2021, https://www.washingtonpost.com/national-security/china-us-talks-anchorage-alaska/2021/03/18/ae2abcfa-880e-11eb-8a67-f314e5fcf88d_story.html.

110 Qu Qiuyan, "Chinese derogatory social media term for 'white left' Western elites spreads," *Global Times*, May 21, 2017, https://www.globaltimes.cn/content/1047989.shtml; and Frankie Huang, "'Baizuo' Is a Chinese Word Conservatives Love," *Foreign Policy*, March 27, 2021,

dedicated to influencing narratives and stoking societal tensions abroad, chief among which are the 'Publicity' or Propaganda Department (CCPPD), which has the 'controlling share' of responsibility for media campaigns, and the Central Office of Foreign Propaganda (COFP, or State Council Information Office) which guides 'the foreign-propaganda activities of the multiple government offices whose portfolios touch on foreign matters.'[111]

Although China has been known to use intimidation and cyberattacks to subvert foreign elections, its propaganda apparatus has 'closely studied' successful Russian trolling and disinformation operations which have become favored tactics.[112] For example, the CCP's Propaganda Departments and Cyberspace Affairs Commissions (CACs) employ a '50 cent army' of over two million 'network civilization volunteers' reportedly paid ¥0.50 for every online post, or simply as part of their official duties, and an additional 20 million part-time young zealots recruited from the Communist Youth League (CYL).[113] Combined, they fabricate around 450 million pieces of content on social media each year.[114] Developed over the last two decades, this integrated system of professional and 'grassroots' internet commentators is essentially a troll horde tasked with: gathering intelligence, censoring dissidents,

https://foreignpolicy.com/2021/03/27/baizuo-chinese-conservatives-liberals-decoder-tucker-carlson.

111 Hamilton and Ohlberg, *Hidden Hand*, 14; and Anne-Marie Brady, *China's Propaganda Machine*, (Washington D. C., Wilson Center, October 26, 2015), https://www.wilsoncenter.org/article/chinas-foreign-propaganda-machine.

112 "Taiwan President Says China Interfering in Election 'Every Day,'" *Reuters*, November 19, 2019, https://www.reuters.com/article/us-taiwan-election-idUSKBN1XT145; Yuichiro Kanematsu, "Fears of Chinese Cybermeddling Grow after Cambodia Election," *Nikkei Asia*, August 17, 2018, https://asia.nikkei.com/Spotlight/Century-of-Data/Fears-of-Chinese-cybermeddling-grow-after-Cambodia-election; Colin Packham, "Exclusive: Australia Concluded China Was behind Hack on Parliament, Political Parties – Sources," *Reuters*, September 15, 2019, https://www.reuters.com/article/us-australia-china-cyber-exclusive-idUSKBN1W00VF; "US Security Adviser Claims China Has Taken 'Most Active Role' in Election Meddling," *The Guardian*, September 4, 2020, https://www.theguardian.com/us-news/2020/sep/04/us-security-adviser-china-elections-meddling; Jeff Seldin, "US: Russia, Iran Meddled in November's Election; China Held Back," *VOA*, September 2, 2021, https://www.voanews.com/usa/us-politics/us-russia-iran-meddled-novembers-election-china-held-back; and Elizabeth Chen, "China Learning from Russia's 'Emerging Great Power' Global Media Tactics," *The Jamestown Foundation*, April 20, 2021, https://jamestown.org/program/china-learning-from-russias-emerging-great-power-global-media-tactics.

113 Ryan Fedasiuk, "A Different Kind of Army: The Militarization of China's Internet Trolls," *The Jamestown Foundation*, April 12, 2021, https://jamestown.org/program/a-different-kind-of-army-the-militarization-of-chinas-internet-trolls; and Gary King, Jennifer Pan, Margaret E. Roberts, "How the Chinese Government Fabricates Social Media Posts for Strategic Distraction, Not Engaged Argument," *American Political Science Review*, Vol. 111, No. 3 (2017), 484–501.

114 King, Pan and Roberts, "How the Chinese Government Fabricates Social Media Posts for Strategic Distraction, not Engaged Argument," 484.

amplifying pro-Party messaging, swamping anti-Party messaging with social media bots, hounding opponents, arranging boycotts of Western businesses, inflaming racial tensions, spreading propaganda, influencing public opinion, generating fake news, impersonating Westerners, and generally inciting as much mayhem as possible online.[115]

The CCP's manipulation of traditional media is equally sophisticated. Under the direction of the CCPPD and a host of other agencies, State media outlets have proliferated and expanded their reach to target Chinese and non-Chinese audiences across the world.[116] These TV stations and newspapers produce and distribute their own propaganda, partner with foreign outlets to mask the origins of the pro-Party content (known as the 'borrowing boats to go to sea' strategy), and purchase controlling stakes in Western media companies (known as 'buying the boat').[117] While China has invested heavily in its own film industry, its targeted investment in Hollywood has been remarkably successful with craven American studios 'now bending over backwards to … gain approval from severe Communist Party censors.'[118] Any actors straying from the CCP line face being pressured into making cringing public apologies (John Cena for calling Taiwan a country)[119] or frozen out of further career opportunities (Richard Gere for criticizing Chinese imperialism in Tibet).[120] The ultimate point, as Xi Jinping himself explained, is to use 'innovative outreach methods' to ensure that CCP propaganda reaches 'wherever the readers are, wherever the viewers are' so that the PRC is only ever

portrayed as a civilized country featuring a rich history, ethnic unity, and cultural diversity, and as an Eastern power with good government, a developed economy, cultural prosperity, national unity, and beautiful scenery. China should also be known as a responsible country that advocates peace

115 Xiao Qiang, "Leaked Propaganda Directives And Banned 'Future,'" *China Digital Times*, June 24, 2011, https://chinadigitaltimes.net/2011/06/future-banned-on-sina-weibo-search.

116 Anne-Marie Brady, "Chinese interference: Anne-Marie Brady's full submission," *Newsroom*, May 8, 2019, https://www.newsroom.co.nz/anne-marie-bradys-full-submission.

117 Louisa Lim and Julia Bergin, "Inside China's audacious global propaganda campaign," *The Guardian*, December 7, 2018, https://www.theguardian.com/news/2018/dec/07/china-plan-for -global-media-dominance-propaganda-xi-jinping; Brady, *China's Propaganda Machine*; and "Chinese interference: Anne-Marie Brady's full submission."

118 Erich Schwartzel, *Red Carpet: Hollywood, China, and the Global Battle for Cultural Supremacy* (Penguin, 2022), blurb.

119 Brady Langmann, The Real Reason John Cena Apologized For Calling Taiwan a Country, *Esquire*, May 26, 2021, https://www.esquire.com/entertainment/movies/a36542951/john-cena -apology-china-taiwan-explained/.

120 Schwartzel, *Red Carpet*, 275–276.

and development, safeguards international fairness and justice, [and] makes a positive contribution to humanity.[121]

All such tactics are examples of Chinese 'political warfare' which is 'warfare, period,' and 'a strategic option that is underway all the time.'[122] Indeed, since 1993, the CCP's entire Cerberean strategy of extraction, projection, and subversion has been molded by the realization that geopolitical success under 'high-technology, informatized conditions' is 'determined by whose story rather than whose army wins', and that 'mass weapons, though a deterrent, have been essentially unusable for sixty years, where kinetic force has too often been a recipe for disappointment and reversal.'[123] In practice, this is underpinned by the 'Three Warfares' doctrine encompassing a mutually-reinforcing combination of media, and psychological and legal warfare.[124] Our focus hereafter shall be upon the latter.

2.3 The Unrestricted Lawfare Program

The Chinese lawfare program was first publicized in *Unrestricted Warfare* (1999), a strategy document written by two PLA colonels. It grew from the PRC's assessment of China's military inferiority vis-à-vis the United States as well as their admiration both for the effectiveness of American sanctions against the Iraqi military during the first Gulf War and the powerful legitimating effect of obtaining UN authorization for the use of force.[125] As one of the Three Warfares, lawfare was incorporated into the Political Work Regulations and Guidelines (2003, 2005, 2010) – 'a unique document providing both military and internal Party regulations' – which are of a sort typically concerned with the management of PLA personnel and domestic civilian morale

121 Sarah Cook, Beijing's Global Megaphone: The Expansion of Chinese Communist Party Media Influence since 2017, (Freedom House, 2020), https://freedomhouse.org/report/special-report /2020/beijings-global-megaphone#footnote8_bpgxb1n; *Chinese Government Influence on the U.S. Media Landscape, before the U.S.-China Economic and Security Review Commission* (2017) (Testimony of Sarah Cook), https://www.uscc.gov/sites/default/files/Sarah%20Cook %20May%204th%202017%20USCC%20testimony.pdf.

122 Dean Cheng, "For the Chinese, Political Warfare Is War by Other Means," *The Heritage Foundation*, April 2, 2020, https://www.heritage.org/asia/commentary/the-chinese-political-warfare -war-other-means.

123 M. Taylor Fravel, *Active Defense: China's Military Strategy since 1949* (Princeton: Princeton University Press, 2019), 218; and Stefan Halper, *China: The Three Warfares* (Report prepared for Director, Office of Net Assessment, Office of the Secretary of Defense, Washington, D.C.: May 2013), 25.

124 Dating from at least 1963 – see Goldenziel, "Law as a Battlefield," 1092–1094.

125 Qiao Liang and Wang Xiangsui, *Unrestricted Warfare* (Beijing: PLA Publishing House, February 1999), 160; and Zong Wenshen, *Legal Warfare: Discussion of 100 Examples and Solutions* (Beijing: PLA Publishing House, 2004), 184–186.

in accordance with CCP objectives.[126] That an outward-looking warfare program was incorporated into ostensibly inward-looking regulations 'may be the function of an external stimulus' (i.e. a modernization drive prompted by intensifying competition with the US) and an ever-tighter fusion of the military and civilian spheres in pursuit of Chinese geopolitical aims.[127] This fusion is itself promoted by 'a National Intelligence Law requiring all Chinese entities to share technology and information with the PRC military, intelligence, and security services.'[128]

Regardless, the rapid development of lawfare in recent decades is 'entirely congruent with Chinese strategic culture' and jurisprudential tradition.[129] While the Chinese legal system has been torn between antinomian Confucianism (or Maoism) and totalizing legalism throughout its long history, it 'never developed a rule of law concept' with an independent judiciary and the attendant checks and balances on state power.[130] In stark contrast with Western Marxists, at no point has the CCP displayed any appreciation for the rule of law as 'an unqualified human good' capable at least of ensuring the equal application of rules to ruled and ruler alike.[131] Whichever dynasty or regime happened to be in charge of China, law served neither as an independent ideal of legality nor as a means to guarantee individual freedom or civil society – it was simply another 'instrument of politics and public order' enabling statesmen to rule *by* law or fiat.[132]

Contemporary Chinese law – which resembles a composite of civil, socialist, and customary law – is no exception to this consistent and thoroughgoing instrumentalism.[133] Despite some unduly optimistic appraisals, it is not trend-

126 Elsa Kania, "The PLA's Latest Strategic Thinking on the Three Warfares," *China Brief*, Vol. 16, No. 13 (2016); and Halper, *China: The Three Warfares*, 31, 271.

127 Halper, *China: The Three Warfares*, 31, 273; and Elsa Kania and Lorand Laskai, *Myths and Realities of China's Military-Civil Fusion Strategy* (Washington, D. C.: Center for a New American Security, January 2021), https://s3.us-east-1.amazonaws.com/files.cnas.org/documents/Myths-and-Realities-of-China%E2%80%99s-Military-Civil-Fusion-Strategy_FINAL-min.pdf?mtime=20210127133521&focal=none.

128 *Protecting Critical and Emerging Technologies from Foreign Threats*, (National Counterintelligence and Security Centre (NCSC), October 21, 2021), 2, https://www.dni.gov/files/NCSC/documents/SafeguardingOurFuture/FINAL_NCSC_Emerging%20Technologies_Factsheet_10_22_2021.pdf

129 James Holmes quoted in Halper, *China: The Three Warfares*, 247.

130 Dean Cheng quoted in Charles J. Dunlap, Jr, "Dean Cheng on 'The Challenge of China: Lawfare, Technology & More,'" *Lawfire*, May 3, 2020, https://sites.duke.edu/lawfire/2020/05/03/podcast-dean-cheng-on-the-challenge-of-china-lawfare-technology-more.

131 See Daniel H. Cole, "'An Unqualified Human Good': E.P. Thompson and the Rule of Law," *Journal of Law and Society*, Vol. 28, No. 2 (2001), 177–203.

132 H. Patrick Glenn, *Legal Traditions of the World*, 5th ed. (Oxford: Oxford University Press, 2014), 332; Sterckx, *Chinese Thought from Confucius to Cook Ding*, 125.

133 Dean Cheng, *Winning Without Fighting: Chinese Legal Warfare*, No. 2692 (Washington, D. C.: Heritage Foundation, May 18, 2012), 3.

ing towards 'a kinder, gentler form of communism' with a greater emphasis on human rights but rather an increasingly severe and comprehensive form of legalism with a relentless focus on economic development.[134] As much was confirmed in a recent speech on 'Xi Jinping's Thought on the Rule of Law' by Chen Yixin, Minister of State Security and Secretary-General of the Central Political and Legal Affairs Commission (responsible for 'poli-legal affairs and enforcement'). In it, he declared that Marxism, the CCP's leadership, and the rule of law were synonymous and that China would 'never take the path of the so-called "constitutional government," "separation of powers," and "judicial independence."' Rather, 'the rule of law serves politics,' and in the face of international pressure, it would be 'necessary to use Xi Jinping's thoughts on the rule of law to better use legal tools to protect the country's dignity and core interests.'[135] The aggressive lawfare campaigns being waged by the PRC, then, are simply the tip of a very long and very firm jurisprudential spear.

Given that PRC strategists 'assign equal importance to preparing the legal and physical battlefields,' it is hardly surprising that 'no state in the world currently has a lawfare strategy as sophisticated as China's.'[136] Although lawfare is often rendered into Chinese as '*falu zhan*,' this should not be thought of as a self-standing concept encapsulated within an authoritative definition. Rather, it denotes one form of combat among many whereby law is used strategically either to complement conventional military operations or as an instrument in its own right to advance commercial, political, or geopolitical ends.[137] That *falu zhan* is geared more towards offense than defense can be deduced from its four official purposes: (1) legal deterrence, (2) legal attack, (3) legal counterattack, and (4) legal binding and legal protection (i.e. constraining adversaries with their own legal systems to protect Chinese interests).[138] This is all simply an extension of standard Chinese jurisprudence wherein any and every

134 See, respectively, Glenn, *Legal Traditions of the World*, 348–349; Xu, *Heaven Has Eyes*, 4; Jerome Alan Cohen, foreword to Albert HY Chen, *An Introduction to the Legal System of the People's Republic of China* (Butterworths, 1992), v–vi; Wang Chenguang and Zhang Xianchu, eds., *Introduction to Chinese Law* (Sweet and Maxwell, 1997), v; Elizabeth M. Lynch, "China's Rule of Law Mirage: The Regression of the Legal Profession Since the Adoption of the 2007 Lawyers Law," *George Washington International Law Review*, Vol. 42 (2011), 535–585; and David K. Schneider, "China's New Legalism," *The National Interest*, Vol. 143 (2016), 19–25; and Kittrie, *Lawfare*, 164.

135 Chen Yixin "On Xi Jinping Thought on Rule of Law", translated by Manoj Kewalramani, *Tracking People's Daily*, April 4, 2021, https://trackingpeoplesdaily.substack.com/p/chen -yixin-on-xi-jinping-thought.

136 Cheng, *Winning Without Fighting*, 6; and Goldenziel, "Law as a Battlefield," 1092.

137 Goldenziel, "Law as a Battlefield," 1093; and Halper, *China: The Three Warfares*, 13.

138 Andrés Munoz Mosquera and Nikoleta Chalanouli, "China, an active practitioner of legal warfare," *Lawfire*, February 2, 2020, https://sites.duke.edu/lawfire/2020/02/02/guest-post-andres -munoz-mosqueras-and-nikoleta-chalanoulis-essay-china-an-active-practitioner-of-legal-war- fare/#_ftn29.

society is a battlefield, and international organizations are mere vessels for PRC *Weltpolitik*.[139] Indeed, the CCP's 'efforts to precondition and control the activities of its opponents through the law often are difficult to differentiate from ordinary administration chores.'[140] Accordingly, there appears to be no centralized department dedicated to *falu zhan* – lawfare is a natural part of the normal functioning of each branch (domestic or foreign, civilian or military) of the state's apparatus. Initially approved by both the Communist Party Central Committee (CPCC) and the Central Military Commission (CMC), geopolitical lawfare is chiefly operationalized by the Ministry of Foreign Affairs, the Political Work Department (a political and propaganda organ of the CMC), the United Front Work Department (the intelligence and influence organ of the CPCC), and the PLA's Strategic Support Force (SSF).[141] The latter 'is a theater command-level organization established [in 2015] to centralize the PLA's strategic space, cyber, electronic, information, communications, and psychological warfare missions and capabilities.'[142] Its Network Systems Department carries out missions associated with the Three Warfares and can mobilize 'new-type militias' composed of technologically competent civilians to supplement these operations.[143] The SSF is officially described as 'a new-type combat force' for 'optimizing the military's force structure and improving integrated support capabilities' via 'system integration [and] military-civilian integration.'[144]

This bureaucratic overlap could be interpreted as a sign of inefficiency and poor coordination, but it should not obscure the fact that the PRC will 'leverage all assets available to the government' for its lawfare efforts: issuing a plethora of dedicated texts and translations of Dunlap, instituting specialized training courses for military personnel and law students, improving the competitiveness of Chinese teams in international moot competitions, providing international scholarships and founding English-language law journals to broadcast CCP talking points to Western academics, and instructing local government and scientific research institutes to engage in lawfare against any perceived threat.[145] The primary vectors of attack can be gleaned from

139 Goldenziel, "Law as a Battlefield," 1091–1092.

140 Mosquera and Chalanouli, "China, an active practitioner of legal warfare."

141 See Kittrie, *Lawfare*, 162; Li-wen Tung, "Taiwan and the CCP's 'Public Opinion Warfare,'" *Taiwan* Strategists, Vol. 2 (2019), 39–60; and Kanchana Ramanujam, "From Human Wave to Info Wave: China's Propaganda Warfare," *CLAWS*, July 3, 2019.

142 Office of the Secretary of Defense, "Military and Security Developments Involving the PRC: Annual Report to Congress 2021" (US Department of Defense, 2021), 64–65, 133.

143 *2022 Report to Congress* (U.S.-China Economic and Security Review Commission (USCC), November 2022), 444–445.

144 Adam Ni and Bates Gill, "The People's Liberation Army Strategic Support Force: Update 2019," *China Brief: Jamestown Foundation*, Vol. 19, No. 10 (2019).

145 Chen Tai Fu and Weng Huai Nan, "Xi'an zheng yuan kaishe falu zhan zhuanti jiaoxue falu zhan zou jin xiandai ketang (西安政院 开设法律战专题教学 法律战走进现代课堂)" [Peoples

the CCP's strategic use of state funding to incentivize legal research that is 'useful for the Party and the government in their decision-making' as regards 'China's overall economic and social development.'[146] Tellingly, the top three 'Recommended Topics' (2009–2014) and 'Funded Proposals' (2007–2014) for Chinese international lawyers are: (1) International Economic Law, (2) Law of the Sea, and (3) International Environmental Law.[147] The disproportionate concentration of resources in these sub-fields is intended to assist CCP economic foreign policy; promote PRC territorial and narrative claims; and ensure Chinese international lawyers can overwhelm and outperform the few Western specialists with expertise in these areas.[148]

Thus, every imaginable instrument, in every imaginable forum, at every imaginable stage of the legal process is used offensively and defensively: 'domestic legislation, international law, judicial law, legal pronouncements, law enforcement and legal education.'[149] Given the 'nearly unlimited expanse of what the [CCP] considers threatening,' the applications and targets of Chinese lawfare are as varied as they are creative.[150] Article 2 of the National Security Law 2015 treats party and state as synonymous when specifying that:

> [N]ational security refers to the relative absence of international or domestic threats to the state's power to govern, sovereignty, unity and territorial integrity, the welfare of the people, sustainable economic and social development, and other major national interests, and the ability to ensure a continued state of security.[151]

Liberation Army University of Defense School of Politics Xi'an Campus opens new course on 'legal warfare.' 'Legal warfare' course enters modern classrooms.] *People's Daily*, May 31, 2004, https://perma.cc/JC89-VHTX; Halper, *China: The Three Warfares*, 70; Kittrie, *Lawfare*, 162–163, 187; Anthea Roberts, *Is International Law International?* (Oxford: Oxford University Press, 2017), 250–254, 278; Matt Sawers, "How Beijing's Cyber Security Engagement Incorporates The Three Warfares," *Australian Outlook*, February 21, 2018, https://www.int ernationalaffairs.org.au/australianoutlook/china-three-warfares-in-cybersecurity; and Anthony Cordesman, Ashley Hess and Nicholas Yaros, *Chinese Military Modernization and Force Development: A Western Perspective,* (Washington, D.C.: Center for Strategic and International Studies, September 2013), 297.

146 Wang Xiaohui (Deputy Head of the CCPPD) quoted in Roberts, *Is International Law International?*, 226.

147 Ibid, 227.

148 Ibid, 228–230.

149 Halper, *China: The Three Warfares*, 29; and Cheng, *Winning Without Fighting*, 2.

150 Peter Mattis, "China's 'Three Warfares' in Perspective," *War on the* Rocks, January 30, 2018, https://warontherocks.com/2018/01/chinas-three-warfares-perspective.

151 Ibid.

The Cerberean method of unrestricted lawfare is deployed against all of these threats. Extractive lawfare is used to acquire required resources and other concessions from adversaries. For example, China trails the West in manufacturing semiconductors (chips) which are 'the DNA of technology' essential to 'all segments of the economy' and underpin 'state-of-the-art military systems.'[152] To offset its dependency on imported chips, the CCP is aggressively exploiting free trade laws the world over to acquire, through state-backed firms, control of the supply chain through ownership of key Western companies. It has also identified 35 strategic 'chokepoint technologies' and is desperately trying to establish domestic industries in these import-dominated areas to insulate itself from Western restrictions on these supply chains.[153]

While intensifying investments by US firms and venture-capital funds in Chinese semiconductor manufacturers are 'aiding Beijing's bid for chip-sector dominance,' the UK's largest chip-manufacturer, Newport Wafer Fab (NWF), which develops technology for fighter aircraft, was initially allowed to be purchased in full by a foreign subsidiary of a Chinese entity despite regulatory scrutiny.[154] Only after considerable vacillation and multiple reviews did the UK government order a partial divestment on national security grounds.[155] Similarly, 10% of Artificial Intelligence (AI) research labs run by US-based companies such as Facebook, Google, IBM, and Microsoft are now housed in China and staffed by 'hundreds of Chinese engineers' – 'indirectly benefitting the Chinese military' through the Military-Civilian Fusion policy or even directly so under 'laws that legally oblige tech companies to hand over their data and any recognized security vulnerabilities.'[156] Such has been the scale of China's success in this sector, and the naivety or unscrupulousness of companies such as Google which simultaneously refuse to work with Western militaries, that the Pentagon's first chief software officer resigned in

152 "Protecting Critical and Emerging Technologies from Foreign Threats," 1; and George Calhoun, "The U.S. Still Dominates In Semiconductors; China Is Vulnerable (Pt 2)," *Forbes*, October 11, 2021, https://www.forbes.com/sites/georgecalhoun/2021/10/11/the-us-still-dominates-in-semiconductors-china-is-vulnerable-pt-2/?sh=74c5105170f7.

153 Calder Walton, *Spies: The Epic Intelligence War Between East and West* (Abacus, 2023), 502.

154 Kate O'Keeffe, Heather Somerville, and Yang Jie, "U.S. Companies Aid China's Bid for Chip Dominance Despite Security Concerns," *The Wall Street Journal*, November 12, 2021, https://www.wsj.com/articles/u-s-firms-aid-chinas-bid-for-chip-dominance-despite-security-concerns-11636718400; and Radomir Tylecote, "Chip Race with China," *The Critic*, November 2, 2021, https://thecritic.co.uk/chip-race-with-china.

155 Decision, *Acquisition of Newport Wafer Fab by Nexperia BV: notice of final order*, (Department for Business, Energy & Industrial Strategy, November 16, 2022), https://www.gov.uk/government/publications/acquisition-of-newport-wafer-fab-by-nexperia-bv-notice-of-final-order.

156 Klon Kitchen and Bill Drexel, "Pull US AI Research Out of China," *Defense One*, August 10, 2021, https://www.defenseone.com/ideas/2021/08/pull-us-ai-research-out-china/184359.

protest and despair.[157] In supply chains already dominated by China, such as the rare metals industry, the CCP is using lawfare to leverage its advantage to extract political concessions from adversaries and ensure that the US military remains 'particularly vulnerable to rare earth lawfare' given its shortfalls in this sector and China's willingness to restrict exports.[158]

All of this works in conjunction with projective lawfare which is used to assert the CCP's power over and against its enemies. To give a range of examples from within China's domestic jurisdiction, the PRC's first Marriage Law (1950) was conceived of by Mao as a 'weapon with which to fight the feudal family system' and consanguineous clan structures which represented a rival powerbase to Party rule.[159] Providing for the liberalization of divorce and abolition of traditional marriage customs, and since consolidated via successor legislation abolishing first cousin marriage, it has proved remarkably successful in its original aim.[160] More recently the CCP has launched a 'judicial blitzkrieg across the country,' arresting and discrediting academics and attorneys accused of 'smearing' the CCP and 'creating social chaos' by acting against the government on sensitive cases.[161] It has also arrested foreign citizens for alleged crimes committed abroad, and its officials generate visa problems for Uyghurs in foreign countries to get them deported back to China.[162]

In the commercial sector it has sought to curtail the growing influence of Chinese tech firms and foreign-owned ventures by accusing them of violating anti-monopoly and data security rules while issuing new guidelines in these areas.[163] Fearing a 'brain drain' from these sectors, 'Beijing has had to impose

---

157 "China has won AI battle with U.S., Pentagon's ex-software chief says," *Reuters*, October 11, 2021. https://www.reuters.com/technology/united-states-has-lost-ai-battle-china-pentagons-ex -software-chief-says-2021-10-11.

158 Kittrie, *Lawfare*, 188–189.

159 Chen Xinxin, "Marriage Law Revisions Reflect Social Progress in China," *China Today*, No. 3 (2001).

160 See the forthcoming Patrick S. Nash, 'Comparative Consanguinity Law: A Global Study of Cousin Marriage Regulations' in Rebecca Probert and Sharon Thompson, *Elgar Research Handbook on Law: Marriage and Cohabitation* (Edward Elgar, 2024).

161 Kittrie, *Lawfare*, 164.

162 Bradley A. Thayer and Lianchao Han, "The growing threat of China's lawfare," *The Hill*, April 9, 2021, https://thehill.com/opinion/international/546811-the-growing-threat-of-chinas-law fare; and Helen Davidson, "Chinese agents operating abroad to get Uyghurs deported, ICC told," *The Guardian*, November 11, 2021, https://www.theguardian.com/world/2021/nov/11/chinese-agents-operating -abroad-to-get-uyghurs-deported-icc-told.

163 Niall Ferguson, "China's Attacks on Tech Are a Losing Strategy in Cold War II," *Bloomberg*, July 11, 2021, https://www.bloomberg.com/opinion/articles/2021-07-11/china-s-attacks-on -didi-alibaba-are-losing-strategy-in-cold-war-against-u-s?sref=ojq9DljU; and Ambrose Evans-Pritchard, "Western investors are 'roadkill' in China's war against its own tech giants," *The Telegraph*, July 28, 2021, https://www.telegraph.co.uk/business/2021/07/28/western-investors -road-kill-chinas-war-against-tech-giants.

emigration restrictions' on domestic talent to stop key workers from leaving for the West.[164] Further, its most recent Counter-Espionage Law (2023) and Foreign Relations Law (2023) target 'ordinary business practices, such as gathering information on local markets, potential partners, and competitors' in order to suppress 'any negative information about China, including its economy.'[165] These are reinforced by the Foreign State Immunity Law (2023) which is 'the first comprehensive PRC legislation dealing specifically with state immunity' and departs from China's longstanding doctrine of absolute state immunity by creating a new exception for 'commercial activity.'[166] This is essentially 'a tool to attack [rival states] on multiple fronts' by enabling civil litigation to be brought against their commercial activities and property under Chinese jurisdiction in retaliation for restricting Chinese investment or transacting military equipment for anti-PRC purposes.[167]

On the international stage, the PRC wages lawfare to expand its horizontal and vertical territorial sovereignty. Best known are its attempts to stake terrestrial and maritime claims in the South China Sea by building upon, and sending militia and weaponized civilian vessels disguised as non-combatants to, disputed islands, all while defending the legitimacy of these annexations under international law via the relevant fora.[168] Any adverse outcomes are immediately countered with vociferous denunciations and continued non-compliance, just as any foreign sanctions are met with rafts of anti-sanctions laws targeting foreign individuals and entities.[169] However, the PRC now also claims that its 'borders extend indefinitely upward through outer space and that all the space within those perimeters is China's sovereign territory.'[170] It is also subjecting private satellite companies to hostile takeover bids and vexatious litigation in order to gain an advantage in low-earth-orbit (LEO) communications technology and military hardware.[171] These moves are motivated

---

164 Calder Walton, *Spies: The Epic Intelligence War Between East and West* (Abacus, 2023), 514.

165 Jay Newman, "China's Coming Lawfare Offensive," *Financial Times*, September 13, 2023.

166 "The implication of the Foreign State Immunity Law on cross-border disputes in the PRC and Hong Kong," *Allen & Overy*, December 20, 2023, https://www.allenovery.com/en-gb/global/news-and-insights/publications/the-implication-of-the-foreign-state-immunity-law-on-cross-border-disputes-in-the-prc-and-hong-kong.

167 Anushka Saxena, "Restricting Foreign State Immunity: China's New Law and What It Means," *The Diplomat*, September 7, 2023, https://thediplomat.com/2023/09/restricting-foreign-state-immunity-chinas-new-law-and-what-it-means/.

168 Kittrie, *Lawfare*, 165–172.

169 Goldenziel, "Law as a Battlefield," 1118–1128; Sydney H. Mintzer, Tamer A. Soliman, Yoshihide Ito, Heng Li and Jing Zhang, "China Passes Broad New Anti-Sanctions Law to Counter Foreign Government Sanctions," *Mayer Brown Blog*, June 16, 2021, https://www.mayerbrown.com/en/perspectives-events/publications/2021/06/china-passes-broad-new-anti-sanctions-law-to-counter-foreign-government-sanctions.

170 Kittrie, *Lawfare*, 168.

171 Glenn Chafetz and Xavier Ortiz, China, Lawfare, and the Contest for Control of Low Earth Orbit, *The Diplomat*, August 10, 2023, https://thediplomat.com/2023/08/china-lawfare-and-the-contest-for-control-of-low-earth-orbit/.

both by the strategic imperative of achieving 'comprehensive national power' on every frontier – space generates economic and technological benefits, contributes to China's global prestige and is critical to control over the communications and information realm – and by the fear of repeating late medieval China's mistake of neglecting its revolutionary sea power capabilities in the face of Western expansion.[172] Thus, the paucity of international treaties governing space and lunar activities – most of which date to the Cold War era – is viewed in Beijing as an opportunity to 'prepare the environment' and 'shape the battlefield' so that the regulation of the space realm favors the PRC and disadvantages its rivals.[173] Accordingly, staking out unlimited vertical sovereignty is intended to deny airspace to Western powers while its attempts to dominate 'a new and broad treaty covering many aspects of outer space law' aims to neutralize American power projection capabilities given that the 'U.S. military relies upon space for 70–90 percent of its intelligence and 80 percent of its communications.'[174]

Cyberspace is yet another domain for PRC lawfare in which it supplies cheap but compromised telecommunications technology to the developing and Western worlds; aggressively undertakes hacking operations in violation of its own agreement with the US which prohibits intentional economic cyber-theft; harvests data and potential kompromat on Western citizens through apps such as TikTok; and attempts to deny the jurisdiction of the international law of armed conflict (LOAC) over the cyber realm in which '95% of the U.S. military's cyber communications network is connected to the internet.'[175] If this latter claim gains legitimacy, it would validate indiscriminate cyberattacks against the global Internet as well as civilian transport, medical and engineering infrastructure; even if it does not, but the US considers itself bound by LOAC in cyberspace while China does not, any American response to kinetic or cyber-attacks would be severely constrained.[176] The PRC is, in sum,

stealing the West's best weapons systems using keystrokes rather than the use of force. It is also positioning itself to shut down the West's critical electrical and other infrastructure without bombing a single power plant. In addition, it is developing the means to revolutionize the brink and conduct of any future kinetic conflict through the hyper-personalization of war, in

172 Dean Cheng, "China and Space: The Next Frontier of Lawfare," *US Institute of Peace*, August 2, 2023.
173 Ibid.
174 White, "Reordering the Law for a China World Order," 453, 460.
175 Orde F. Kittrie, "Chinese Lawfare in the Maritime, Aviation, and Information Technology Domains" *SSRN* (2022), 10–16; and *Lawfare*, 168–172.
176 Ibid.; White, "Reordering the Law for a China World Order," 466–485.

which it would deploy financial, health, and other personalized data about Western troops to blackmail, distract, and demoralize individual Western warfighters and their families.[177]

As well as projecting its own power through lawfare, the CCP uses it to subvert its enemies' institutions and morale. Anything or anyone associated with the 'rules-based international order' is a potential target. For example, the PRC has consistently and deliberately neglected to implement or enforce binding economic and non-proliferation sanctions on allied rogue nations such as Iran and North Korea.[178] Further, it has infiltrated key international organizations either to destroy their credibility or repurpose them for spreading CCP propaganda. This can be seen in the placing of undue pressure on World Bank officials to skew data in favor of China by the current Managing Director of the International Monetary Fund (IMF), Kristalina Georgieva; in the statements of the Director-General of the World Health Organization (WHO), Tedros Adhanom Ghebreyesus, which 'almost directly' mirrored those of the CCP as it sought to deflect blame for the COVID-19 pandemic; and in the PRC's evolution into 'a highly effective player' capable of taking an 'increasingly assertive and proactive stance' within international organizations by, for example, getting itself elected to the United Nations Human Rights Council and using it to 'slander and smear' its critics.[179] Elsewhere it has simply created a series of international financial institutions (namely the Asian Infrastructure Investment Bank and the New Development Bank) to rival established agencies such as the World Bank and the International Monetary Fund.[180] To complement these efforts, the Supreme People's Court (SPC) has created two branches of the International Commercial Court of China (CICC) to dispose of disputes arising from the Belt and Road Initiative under Chinese law.[181]

177 Kittrie, "Chinese Lawfare in the Maritime, Aviation, and Information Technology Domains," 1.
178 Kittrie, *Lawfare*, 173–183.
179 Andrea Shalal and David Lawder, "IMF chief called out over pressure to favor China while at World Bank," *Reuters*, September 17, 2021, https://www.reuters.com/business/sustainable-business/world-bank-kills-business-climate-report-after-ethics-probe-cites-undue-pressure-2021-09-16; Kathy Gilsinan, "How China Deceived the WHO," *The Atlantic*, April 12, 2020, https://www.theatlantic.com/politics/archive/2020/04/world-health-organization-blame-pandemic-coronavirus/609820; and Sophie Richardson, "China's 'Slanders and Smears' at UN Human Rights Council," *Human Rights Watch*, March 11, 2021, https://www.hrw.org/news/2021/03/11/chinas-slanders-and-smears-un-human-rights-council; Kittrie, *Lawfare*, 187.
180 Goldenziel, "Law as a Battlefield," 1038–1040.
181 Jue Jun Lu, "Dispute resolution along the Belt and Road: what does the future hold?" *Thomson Reuters Practical Law Arbitration* Blog, August 2, 2018, http://arbitrationblog.practicallaw.com/dispute-resolution-along-the-belt-and-road-what-does-the-future-hold; and Nyshka Chandran, "China's plans for creating new international courts are raising fears of bias,"

The 'leading edge' of Three Warfares operations is directed against Taiwan, whose 2020 elections were hit with an 'aggressive disinformation campaign' and which is currently subject to the Anti-Secession Law (2005) which signals to the world that the PRC is self-authorized to take 'non-peaceful and other necessary actions' to accomplish 'reunification.'[182] This especially intensive Chinese lawfare campaign seeks 'to reframe the relationship between Beijing and Taipei as an internal dispute, to close down Taiwan's international space and to contain any right to self-determination.'[183] Within the West itself, PRC-linked organizations are known to threaten or launch civil lawsuits against critics, while Huawei, the Chinese telecommunications company with 'a history of industrial espionage and close ties to the CCP,' is locked in a protracted legal battle with the US government over spying allegations.[184]

Diverse as all these examples from each Cerberean head are, they all feed into a broader information/narrative strategy designed to spread and strengthen the CCP's political agenda; protect and enhance the Party's reputation; transform disputed geopolitical claims into accepted facts on the ground; distract and divide adversaries while curtailing their military effectiveness; and preparing the battlefield – legal, cyber, intelligence, geopolitical, kinetic, societal – to favor the forces of the PRC.[185] The point is less about the outcome of a particular legal contest and more about attaining ultimate victory against an opponent.[186] Now that it has 'the third largest number of lawyers in the world' – many of whom are fluent in English and possess higher degrees from Western universities[187] – and is perhaps the world's most 'shrewd, savvy, and successful operator,' there is every reason to expect China to become even

CNBC, February 1, 2018, https://www.cnbc.com/2018/02/01/china-to-create-international-courts-for-belt-and-road-disputes.html.

182 Sean Quirk, "Lawfare in the Disinformation Age: Chinese Interference in Taiwan's 2020 Elections," *Harvard International Law Journal*, Vol. 62 No. 2 (2021), 525; and You Ji, "China's anti-secession law and the risk of war in the Taiwan Strait," *Contemporary Security Policy*, Vol. 27, No. 2 (2006), 237–257.

183 Michael West and Aurelio Insisa, "Reunifying Taiwan with China through Cross-Strait Lawfare," *China Quarterly* (2023), 1.

184 Hai Yan, "China Backs Lawsuits Against German Scholar for Human Rights Abuse Claims," *VOA*, March 16, 2021, https://www.voanews.com/east-asia-pacific/voa-news-china/china-backs-lawsuits-against-german-scholar-human-rights-abuse; Patrick Turner, "China's Largest Telecom May Sue You For Criticizing It," *Defense One*, November 26, 2019, https://www.defenseone.com/policy/2019/11/chinas-largest-telecom-may-sue-you-criticizing-it/161564; Ruo Zhang, "China considers suing rumor-mongering researchers and think tanks for libel," *Global Times*, August 7, 2021, https://www.globaltimes.cn/content/1193872.shtml; and Goldenziel, "Law as a Battlefield," 1130–1136.

185 Goldenziel, "Law as a Battlefield," 1092–1093; Kittrie, *Lawfare*, 161–163; and Tung, "Taiwan and the CCP's 'Public Opinion Warfare,'" 42.

186 Cheng, *Winning Without Fighting*, 6.

187 Roberts, *Is International Law International?*, 250.

'more adept at waging lawfare over the coming decades.'[188] Having diligently crafted what might be termed 'unrestricted lawfare with Chinese characteristics,' the CCP has at its disposal a formidable doctrine underpinned by ancient strategic and jurisprudential traditions, extremely creative and versatile in its application, well-resourced and institutionalized at every level, entirely unconstrained by ethical qualms or constitutional norms, and increasingly effective at scale against a range of targets. And yet.

2.4 Strategic Threat Assessment

As Master Sun Tzu advised his students, 'Know the enemy, know yourself, and victory is never in doubt, not in a hundred battles,' so the Master Detective advises his:

> on meeting a fellow mortal, learn at a glance to distinguish the history of the man, and the trade or profession to which he belongs. Puerile as such an exercise may seem, it sharpens the faculties of observation, and teaches one where to look and what to look for.[189]

Accordingly, the foregoing study sought to render Chinese lawfare legible to Western inquirers in its own right and on its own terms. By setting the doctrine of unrestricted lawfare within its own rich cultural and historical context, it is hoped that the reader departs with a newfound appreciation for its depth and sophistication but also for its inherent pitfalls and the fallibility of its executors. After all, like any nation of fellow mortals and even Moriarty himself, the PRC is more than capable of making 'colossal errors' which its enemies can exploit.[190]

Not least among them is the CCP's fundamental inability – 'despite its enormous economic power' and unlike the Soviets – to entice idealistic converts (as opposed to the occasional venal wretch) to the racialized 'China dream' with its parody of human rights and democracy.[191] There is certainly evidence to suggest that the CCP is 'failing in its mission to sway global public opinion of China' and that its aggressive political warfare is proving counterproductive.[192] For example, a 2018 Pew Foundation poll of 25 countries found that only 19% thought that Chinese hegemony would be better for the world, while across Asia and in those European countries where China

---

188 Kittrie, *Lawfare*, 186–187.
189 Quoted in Paul R. Viotti and Mark V. Kauppi, *International Relations Theory*, 6th ed. (Lanham, Md.: Rowman & Littlefield, 2020), 245; and Doyle, *A Study in Scarlet*.
190 Pitron, *The Rare Metals War*, 11.
191 Ibid.; Andrew, *The Secret World*, 68; and Hayton, *The Invention of China*, 182.
192 Fedasiuk, "A Different Kind of Army."

has been most active – Spain, France, Greece, and Italy – polling revealed the lowest levels of confidence in Xi Jinping's leadership and the highest levels of mistrust as regards the CCP's respectfulness towards personal freedoms.[193] Unfavorable views of China are now at 'historic highs' across the West and have become more widespread with each passing year.[194] Even *tianxia*, the CCP's heavily propagated Sinocentric alternative to the Westphalian rules-based international order, is increasingly regarded as a transparent 'trope' lacking any 'compelling incentives for major players in the current international system.'[195] After all, and despite its 'efforts to educate the world on the virtues of a Confucian Great Harmony,' the PRC has itself come to tacitly accept many Westphalian principles, having joined the UN and whenever it 'zealously defends its sovereign prerogatives' against external interference.[196]

Likewise, United Front events are reportedly suffering from poor attendance and still only hold a 'minority appeal' among the estimated 60 million overseas Chinese.[197] The most recent and authoritative study of the CCP's 'global media offensive' considers it a 'stumbling' and 'uneven' success at best, and bluntly concludes that 'Doomsayers suggesting Beijing's influence is, right now, exceptionally skillful and effective are wrong.'[198] What is more, surrounding countries subject to the CCP's relentless attacks are beginning to improve their own lawfare capabilities and mount retaliatory lawfare campaigns.[199] This is especially true in the South China Sea where support for China's territorial claims 'is waning' and 'it has not succeeded in creating the presumption that Chinese enforcement of its invalidated claims is anywhere near legality.'[200] And all this despite the CCP's heavy investment in strategic research, legal training, and compliant international law journals.[201]

Crucially, however, the PRC's Three Warfares doctrine is starting to provoke an 'intense blowback' as its adversaries adapt and cooperate more closely

193 Economy, *The Third Revolution*, 223–224.
194 Elizabeth C. Economy, *The World According to China* (Cambridge: Polity, 2022), 20.
195 June Teufel Dreyer, "The 'Tianxia Trope': will China change the international system?" *Journal of Contemporary China*, Vol. 24, No. 96 (2015), pp. 1015–1031.
196 Ibid.
197 Hayton, *The Invention of China*, 100.
198 Joshua Kurlantzick, *Beijing's Global Media Offensive: China's Uneven Campaign to Influence Asia and the World* (Oxford: Oxford University Press, 2023), 10.
199 Jill Goldenziel, "The Truth About The Philippines' New Strategy Against China," *Forbes*, March 30, 2023, https://www.forbes.com/sites/jillgoldenziel/2023/03/30/the-truth-about-the-philippines-new-strategy-against-china/; Charmaine Misalucha-Willoughby, "Small States Wield Nationalism and Lawfare to Navigate Great-Power Competition," *Issue Brief*, No. 626 (Observer Research Foundation, March 2023).
200 Christian Schultheiss, "What Has China's Lawfare Achieved in the South China Sea?" *ISEAS Perspective*, 2, https://www.iseas.edu.sg/wp-content/uploads/2023/06/ISEAS_Perspective_2023_51.pdf.
201 Roberts, *Is International Law International?*, 240–254.

to thwart Chinese ambitions.[202] No longer distracted by the decades-long War on Terror and having forged multilateral security partnerships such as Quad Plus (Australia, India, Japan, US, New Zealand, South Korea, Vietnam) and AUKUS (Australia, UK, US), the West is increasingly fixated on the threat posed by the CCP. As Peter Thiel recently put it in relation to pro-CCP sentiment in Western institutions (i.e. universities, Silicon Valley, Hollywood, Wall Street), 'that train has left,' and it is no longer in their self-interest 'to be picking up pennies in front of a bulldozer.'[203] Equally threatening to the PRC's economic prospects are its 'new laws and regulations that seek to bend investors to the ruling party's priorities and render overseas regulators irrelevant... If the CCP wages lawfare on Western companies, as now appears likely, the economic fallout will be massive.'[204] These measures – which include forcing top bankers to devote 'a third of working time to study Xi Thought' – will soon force Western companies to choose between (1) writing off investments in China to comply with the transparency and due diligence requirements of Western regulators; or (2) complying with Chinese security regulations to 'go dark' to independent assessment and 'risk multimillion dollar fines and liability' from Western regulators. Unsurprisingly, confidence in the Chinese economy has 'taken a hit' as 'they cannot do both,' and Western shareholder derivative lawyers are already being advised to 'sharpen your knives.'[205]

Further, the degree to which China's legal system has been politicized and subordinated to the CCP, for example, has created unprecedented scope for corruption. Although hard to verify, confidence in the Chinese legal system appears to be suffering at home and abroad – dangerous prospects indeed for China's ruling elite.[206] While it is inherently difficult to obtain accurate information on corruption within the Party and State, evidence from China's commercial sector indicates that rapid expansion and overlapping bureaucracy has resulted in 'enormous inefficiency, waste, and fraud.'[207] Such concerns are one of the best explanations for changes to the CCP's diplomatic behavior over time, as its leadership plays a 'two-level game' in which aggres-

202 Ibid.; see generally Richard McGregor, *Xi Jinping: The Backlash* (Australia: Penguin Books Australia, 2019); and Luke Patey, *How China Loses: The Pushback Against Chinese Global Ambitions* (New York: Oxford University Press, 2021).

203 Peter Thiel, interview, *Peter Thiel: "Diversity Myth" 30 Years Later*, Founders Fund, August 18, 2023, hosted by Mike Solana, https://foundersfund.com/2023/08/diversity-myth-30-years-later/.

204 John Pomfret et al., "Capital Markets with Chinese Characteristics" (FDD, 14 September 2023); Jay Newman, "China's Coming Lawfare Offensive," *Financial Times*, 13 September 2023; "Bankers Forced to Study Xi's Thoughts as Party Tightens Grip," *Bloomberg*, August 8, 2023, https://www.bloomberg.com/news/articles/2023-08-08/bankers-forced-to-study-xi-s-thoughts-as-party-tightens-grip?leadSource=uverify%20wall.

205 Ibid.

206 Kittrie, *Lawfare*, 164.

207 Economy, *The Third Revolution*, 126.

sive international diplomacy is employed to distract from festering domestic problems.[208] Human bureaucracies being what they are, there is every reason to expect that the all-pervasive but diffuse official responsibility for lawfare within the PRC generates vicious internecine jostling and resource squandering, all while hindering inter-agency coordination and the accumulation of institutional expertise that would otherwise occur in a more streamlined institutional environment.[209]

Finally, it is worth noting that the PRC is genuinely and seriously afraid of retaliatory lawfare for good reason. Despite the Chinese predominance in rare earth metals, the global supply of hyper-pure silicon required for advanced semiconductors can only be mined from a single seam of pristine quartz located in North Carolina and protected by hyper-secure facilities. As Ed Conway notes, the US therefore exerts incontestable control over this critical raw material and a growing global industry that is 'utterly reliant on a single place.'[210] China has 'tried [and failed] for decades to produce quartz of a similar standard,' so the CCP is extremely sensitive to any restrictions imposed upon any aspect of the semiconductor supply chain.[211] Tellingly, as Chris Miller relates at the beginning of *Chip War*, even as the *USS Mustin* sailed through the Taiwan Strait in August 2020, the CCP was 'less worried about the US Navy and more about an obscure US Commerce Department regulation called the Entity List, which limits the transfer of American technology abroad.'[212] Having added Huawei to the List, the US effectively precluded it from purchasing vital semiconductors made with US technology, and the firm's 'global expansion ground to a halt' as 'revenue slumped' without recovering.[213] Trailing Australia, New Zealand, and Japan, the UK eventually followed suit by banning Huawei technology from 5G public networks and ordering its complete removal before 2028 'due to the impact of US sanctions on its supply chain.'[214]

208 Robert D. Putnam, "Diplomacy and domestic politics: the logic of two-level games," *International Organization*, Vol. 42, No. 3 (1988), 427–460; and Lee Jones, "The myth of monolithic China," *Unherd*, September 9, 2021, https://unherd.com/2021/09/the-myth-of-monolithic-china/?s=08.

209 See generally Lee Jones and Shahar Hameiri, *Fractured China: How State Transformation Is Shaping China's Rise* (Cambridge: Cambridge University Press, 2021).

210 Ed Conway, *Material World: A Substantial Story of our Past and Future* (London: WH Allen, 2023), 105–106.

211 Ibid.

212 Chris Miller, *Chip War: The Fight for the World's Most Critical Technology* (London: Simon & Schuster, 2022), xviii.

213 Ibid.

214 Department for Digital, Culture, Media & Sport and The Rt Hon Michelle Donelan MP, "Huawei legal notices issued," *U.K Government Press Release*, October 13, 2022, https://www.gov.uk/government/news/huawei-legal-notices-issued.

The blacklisting of Huawei was swiftly followed by the US's CHIPS and Science Act 2022, which is intended to 'strengthen American supply chains' via federal incentives and 'counter China' via a raft of 'national security guardrails' which preclude access to these incentives should a semiconductor manufacturer attempt to operate and expand chip production in 'countries of concern' (namely China, Russia, North Korea, and Iran).[215] Throughout 2023, various Western allies began coordinating their export controls on chipmaking equipment (US–Japan–Netherlands) and enforcement regimes (US, UK, Canada, Australia, and New Zealand) in order to 'enhance their effectiveness, minimize gaps and foster joint investigations and coordinated enforcement actions.'[216] Unsurprisingly, the CCP retaliated with a vigorous 'strategic messaging campaign' asserting that these measures violate WTO rules and will backfire against Western companies while spurring the growth of China's domestic semiconductor industry.[217] This vehement reaction clearly indicates that the CCP regards semiconductor lawfare as a serious threat to its geopolitical ambitions and manufacturing economy which remains 'fatally dependent on foreigners to make the chips upon which all modern electronics depend.'[218] As well it might, for to see how this may play out on a real battlefield, one need look no further than Russia's desperate resort to 'primitive Soviet-era munitions' against Ukraine since losing access to Western semiconductors.[219] This gives cause for hope that, impressive and intimidating as it is, unrestricted lawfare is no magic weapon against concerted Western action. What is more, the West is well 'positioned to fight lawfare, and to win.'[220]

215 Biden-Harris Administration, "Fact Sheet: CHIPS and Science Act Will Lower Costs, Create Jobs, Strengthen Supply Chains, and Counter China," *White House Briefing Room*, August 9, 2022, https://www.whitehouse.gov/briefing-room/statements-releases/2022/08/09/fact-sheet-chips-and-science-act-will-lower-costs-create-jobs-strengthen-supply-chains-and-counter-china/.

216 Sujai Shivakumar, Charles Wessner, and Thomas Howell, ""Guardrails" on CHIPS Act Funding to Restrict Investments in China May Restrict Participation in CHIPS Act Incentives," *Centre for Strategic and International Studies (CSIS)*, November 7, 2023, https://www.csis.org/blogs/perspectives-innovation/guardrails-chips-act-funding-restrict-investments-china-may-restrict.

217 S.Z. Tan and Peter W. Singer, "How China Is Trying to Turn the US CHIPS Act to Its Favor," *Defense One*, November 16, 2022, https://www.defenseone.com/ideas/2022/11/how-china-trying-turn-us-chips-act-its-favor/379828/.

218 Miller, *Chip War*, xviii.

219 Zoya Sheftalovich and Laurens Cerulus, "The chips are down: Putin scrambles for high-tech parts as his arsenal goes up in smoke," *Politico*, September 5, 2022.

220 Goldenziel, "Information Lawfare," 799.

3   A Western Way of Total Lawfare

3.1 The Politico-Legal Tradition

American law is as much a product of American ideals as a reflection of the United States as it really is.[1] As the world's preeminent democratic, financial, and military power, and the nation with the greatest number of lawyers per capita, it is entirely unsurprising that the term 'lawfare' should have sprung from the United States Armed Forces.[2] With respect to Dunlap's considerable ingenuity, the (mis)perception that the intellectual history of lawfare begins in Fall 2001 plays into the tropes peddled by America's enemies of a cosmetic, consumeristic society headed for intellectual bankruptcy.[3]

Nothing could be further from the truth, but whereas the Chinese can draw upon millennia of strategic thought and instrumental jurisprudence to inform their practice, American lawyers have taken such little interest in their own common law tradition that they lack the self-confidence and tools to respond. This stasis may last indefinitely absent any serious engagement with Anglo-American jurisprudence, both to illuminate its conceptual richness and assuage contemporary policymakers. The future of Western lawfare depends, in short, on it being accepted as authentically indigenous as apple pie. Such is the task of the pages to follow, which will establish beyond doubt that the emergence of Western lawfare at the turn of the 21st century, like the Reagan Revolution before it and the American Revolution before that, was less of a

---

1 The leading one- and multi-volume histories of United States law are agreed on this much – see Lawrence Friedman, *A History of American Law*, 4th ed. (Oxford: Oxford University Press, 2019); and G. Edward White, *Law in American History*, Vols. I–III (Oxford: Oxford University Press, 2012–2019).

2 J. Mark Ramseyer and Eric B. Rasmusen, "Comparative litigation rates," *The Harvard John M. Olin Discussion Paper Series* (2010); Gillian K. Hadfield, "Higher Demand, Lower Supply – A Comparative Assessment of the Legal Resource Landscape for Ordinary Americans," *Fordham Urban Law Journal*, Vol 37. No. 1 (2010), 129; and "Clements Worldwide Risk Index," *Clements Worldwide*, (Summer/Fall 2016).

3 See Ian Buruma and Avishai Margalit, *Occidentalism: A Short History of Anti-Westernism* (London: Penguin, 2005).

DOI: 10.4324/9781032724003-3

revolution and more like a 'great rediscovery, a rediscovery of our values and our common sense.'[4] It is to the process of rediscovery we must now turn.

Dunlap's 2001 paper is neither the *fons et origio* nor the etymological and semiotic dead-end that conventional histories of lawfare imply. Rather, it is the product of a snapshot in time at the juncture of two worlds. Such times are best described thus: 'The old world is dying, and the new world struggles to be born: now is the time of monsters.'[5] With bombs already falling on the Islamic Emirate of Afghanistan, it was the 'good decade' capping off the American century that was dying. The long 1990s had a particular *zeitgeist* – victory in the Cold War and the Middle East, great prosperity, games consoles, garish fashion, girl bands, third-wave feminism, *Friends* and *Frasier*, Crystal Pepsi, the O.J. trial, MTV – in which Western governments basked in the end of history and occupied themselves by tinkering with the economy, stupid. That passed on 9/11, and the monster responsible for killing it, radical Islam, was in time joined by others, not least a Putinizing Russia, and, though few saw it at the time, the increasingly mighty People's Republic of China. All three remain with us to this day, taking advantage of new technologies and creeping postmodernism to weaponize truth itself, flooding the internet and other media with disinformation as cover for cyber, economic, kinetic, and hybrid attacks on the US and its allies.[6]

Late 2001 in America, then, with urgency and outrage pulsing through the nation, was the perfect time and place to open up a brave new world of war. Even so, that new world was built on more than an atrocity and did not rise fully formed from Ground Zero. Whether or not Dunlap realized it at the time, the raw materials from which he forged lawfare were homegrown and far older than the American primacy he strove to protect. Understanding how they came together, and reclaiming a rich intellectual heritage, is as interesting an exercise in applied history as it is a vital prerequisite to mastering the techniques, applications, and implications of future lawfare campaigns. The story has two strands, jurisprudential and geopolitical, which shall be taken in turn.

The 'law' component of lawfare, fittingly enough, has its roots in some of America's earlier wars. The first distinctively American jurisprudence was that of the legal realists. Their movement reached its zenith under Oliver Wendell Holmes Jr. (1841–1935) – the realist from whom all realists derive[7] – and Karl Llewellyn (1893–1962) – the 'best known and most substantial

---

4 President Ronald Reagan quoted in Gil Troy, *The Reagan Revolution: A Very Short Introduction* (Oxford: Oxford University Press, 2009), blurb.

5 Antonio Gramsci quoted in Slavoj Žižek, "A Permanent Economic Emergency," *New Left Review*, Vol. 64 (July/August 2010).

6 See Pomerantsev, *This Is Not Propaganda*.

7 Karl Llewellyn on Holmes quoted in Roger Cotterrell, *The Politics of Jurisprudence*, 2nd ed. (Oxford: Oxford University Press, 2003), 183.

realist' of all.[8] It is worth noting that both were enthusiastic volunteers who served with distinction and suffered injury during, respectively, the American Civil War and the Great War.[9] Their war years clearly left a mark as American realism – meant in the plain sense of being realistic and worldly about law[10] – was crafted into a pragmatic and unsentimental branch of jurisprudence. Its animating spirit is best captured without elaboration in this famous passage from Holmes's *The Common Law* (1881):

> [T]he life of the law has not been logic: it has been experience. The felt necessities of the time, the prevalent moral and political theories, intuitions of public policy, avowed or unconscious, even the prejudices which judges share with their fellow men, have a good deal more to do than the syllogism in determining the rules by which men should be governed. The law embodies the story of a nation's development through many centuries, and it cannot be dealt with as if it contained only the axioms and corollaries of a book of mathematics. In order to know what it is, we must know what it has been, and what it tends to become.[11]

The proper approach to the practice of law, then, was to step into the mind of 'the bad man' who cares only for the legal knowledge relevant to his case and, more specifically, that which will enable him to predict the material consequences stemming from his actions or intended course of action. This did not necessitate cynicism towards 'the vaguer sanctions of conscience' for 'law is the witness and external deposit of our moral life' – it simply meant that mastering it for intellectual and practical purposes – and for dealing with bad men – required more than moralizing.[12] Good lawyers and lawmakers, in other words, could simultaneously hold fast to their 'internal view' – as to what the law should be, what it should be used for, and how – while adopting, as detached professionals, an 'external view' encompassing what the law was, what it could be used for, and how.[13]

---

8 William Twining, *Karl Llewellyn and the Realist Movement*, 2nd ed. (Cambridge: Cambridge University Press, 2014), blurb.

9 See Stephen Budiansky, *Oliver Wendell Holmes: A Life in War, Law, and Ideas* (New York: Norton, 2020), 72–126; and Twining, *Karl Llewellyn and the Realist Movement*, 535–543.

10 Brian H. Bix, *Jurisprudence: Theory and Context*, 7th ed. (London: Sweet & Maxwell, 2015), 196.

11 Oliver Wendell Holmes Jr., *The Common Law* (Boston: M.D. Howe ed., Little, Brown & Co., 1963), 5.

12 Oliver Wendell Holmes Jr., "The Path of the Law," *Harvard Law Review*, Vol. 10, No. 8 (1897), 457–478.

13 This conceptual distinction was later reformulated with exceptional clarity – see H.L.A. Hart, *The Concept of Law*, 3rd ed. (Oxford: Oxford University Press, 2012), 89–91, 242–243.

These were precisely the practical questions that occupied Karl Llewellyn. Llewellyn's realism, as he put it, 'is not a philosophy – it is a technology.'[14] For him, law was an institution with no 'values in itself' but two basic functions.[15] The first was purely practical: 'to make group survival possible' by 'keeping society (or indeed of any group) together and alive.'[16] The second was idealistic: to 'quest' for efficiency, justice, and the realization of individual and societal aspirations.[17] Around these clustered a set of 'law-jobs,' the most important of which were: (1) the disposition of wrongs, grievances of disputes that might tear the society apart; (2) preventing trouble by channeling conduct and expectations while responding effectively to changing conditions; and (3) organizing society as a whole 'so as to provide integration, direction and incentive.'[18] In short, the business of the law was dealing with conflict and change; the business of legal officials (practitioners, judges, academics, lawmakers, and so on) was to hone their respective crafts so that the institution of law functioned optimally; the business of the realist was to keep one eye open for emerging dangers and the other fixed on institutional purposes.

It is hard to overstate the importance of American legal realism around the turn of the 20th century and, to a lesser extent, down to the present. During its heyday under Holmes, Llewellyn, and others, it became jurisprudential orthodoxy across the United States into which no rival theory could penetrate.[19] Realists staffed the judiciary, dominated legal education, created the Uniform Civil Code, and played a major role in crafting the institutional infrastructure of Roosevelt's New Deal.[20] To them, realism was a self-evident creed for a technological age in which 'getting things done' the American way was so visibly successful in scientific, industrial, and financial terms.[21] It would go on to inspire a raft of derivatives ranging from Law and Economics to Critical Legal Studies.[22] Even today, treating law as a means to an end remains prevalent enough, in theory and practice, to prompt pioneering critiques as well as the cliché 'we are all realists now.'[23]

---

14 Quoted in Raymond Wacks, *Understanding Jurisprudence: An Introduction to Legal Theory*, 5th ed. (Oxford: Oxford University Press, 2017), 168.

15 Karl Llewellyn, "A Realistic Jurisprudence – The Next Step," *Columbia Law Review*, Vol. 30, No. 4 (1930), 431; and Wacks, *Understanding Jurisprudence*, 172.

16 Michael Freeman, *Lloyd's Introduction to Jurisprudence*, 8th ed. (London: Sweet & Maxwell, 2008), 991, 1017.

17 Ibid., 991.

18 Ibid., 1016–1017.

19 Ibid., 824–825.

20 Bix, *Jurisprudence*, 195–204.

21 Cotterrell, *The Politics of Jurisprudence*, 194–199.

22 Freeman, *Lloyd's Introduction to Jurisprudence*, 837.

23 See Brian Z. Tamanaha, *Law as a Means to an End: Threat to the Rule of Law* (Cambridge: Cambridge University Press, 2006), 2–8; and Twining, *Karl Llewellyn and the Realist Movement*, 382

Nevertheless, both Holmes and Llewellyn were conscious of the limits of realism and prescient enough to realize that it would be misrepresented as amoral or worse.[24] Rather than being a comprehensive philosophy of law devoid of moral commitments, it was intended merely as 'a way of looking at legal rules and legal processes.'[25] These rules and processes, not to mention the institutions and practitioners sustaining them, were only an aspect of 'a wider point of view from which the distinction between law and morals becomes of secondary or no importance.'[26] Thus, realism and the realists themselves were as much a product of liberal American society as they were infused with its moral vision which valorized choice, decision, responsibility, accountability, and compartmentalization.[27] Regardless, the dominance of realism eventually collapsed following World War II. This was chiefly due to its perceived obsolescence in the face of H.L.A. Hart's sophisticated positivism and because natural law critics likened it to the technocratic amorality of Nazism in which German judges had been complicit.[28] In the place of realism, an antitotalitarian 'liberalism of fear' gestated in East Coast campuses as the civil rights movement inched forward and yet another war, this time against Communists in Vietnam, moved progressive intellectuals to reimagine law as a vehicle for equality, welfare, and universal rights.[29]

While American realism had never gained much traction outside of the United States, post-war liberal individualism took the world by storm.[30] Following the publication of John Rawls's *A Theory of Justice* in 1971 and Ronald Dworkin's *Taking Rights Seriously* in 1977, it became an axiom of Anglo-American jurisprudence to translate questions of political justice into the language of rights.[31] All manner of problems, from social deprivation at home to murderous dictatorships abroad, began to fall under law's empire, and it became virtually inconceivable to imagine solutions without reference

24 Holmes, "The Path of the Law," 334; and Twining, *Karl Llewellyn and the Realist Movement*, 148.
25 Harry W. Jones, "Law and Morality in the Perspective of Legal Realism," *Columbia Law Review*, Vol. 65, No. 5 (1961), 799.
26 Holmes, "The Path of the Law," 335.
27 Jones, "Law and Morality in the Perspective of Legal Realism," 809.
28 See Brian Leiter, "Legal Realism and Legal Positivism Reconsidered," *Ethics*, Vol. 111, No. 2 (2001), 278–279; and Rodger D. Citron, "The Nuremberg Trials and American Jurisprudence: The Decline of Legal Realism, The Revival of Natural Law, and the Development of Legal Process Theory," *Michigan State Law Review*, No. 2 (2006), 398.
29 See Judith N. Shklar, "The Liberalism of Fear," in Nancy L. Rosenblum, ed., *Liberalism and the Moral Life* (Cambridge, Mass.: Harvard University Press, 1989), 21–29; Paul Kelly, *Liberalism* (Cambridge: Polity Press, 2005), 7; and Michael J. Sandel, *Liberalism and the Limits of Justice*, 2nd ed. (Cambridge: Cambridge University Press, 1998), 1.
30 Cotterrell, *The Politics of Jurisprudence*, 194–199.
31 Mary Ann Glendon, *Rights Talk: The Impoverishment of Political Discourse* (New York: Free Press, 1993); and Nigel Biggar, *What's Wrong with Rights?* (Oxford: Oxford University Press, 2020).

to the ideals of equality and legality. Indeed, on the global stage, the West has sought to promote a 'rules-based international order' via doctrines such as the 'responsibility to protect' (endorsed 2005) and institutions such as the International Criminal Court (opened 2002) and the United Nations Human Rights Council (founded 2006).[32] Even the most squalid regimes have felt the need to pay lip service to these ideals and participate, however cynically, in these American-made institutions.[33] In domestic settings such as the United Kingdom's, this 'golden age of rights' was manifested through the rapid transformation of the uncodified political constitution into an increasingly legalistic one centered upon statutes such as the Human Rights Act 1998.[34] At the same time, the general public's propensity to sue increased after 1970, and the new Supreme Court Justices started to acquire celebrity status in their own right.[35]

To give just one indication of speed and scale, in 1985 the philosopher Alan Ryan concluded his discussion of Rawls by stating that 'British politics is unaccustomed to a strenuous insistence on people's rights'; by 2015 the celebrated campaigner Shami Chakrabarti (as she then was) could plausibly announce, with quasi-religious conviction, that 'human rights are the only truly universal language other than war.'[36] In the space of several decades, then, the language of liberal American jurists became the *lingua franca* of intellectuals and statesmen the world over.[37] And yet. That legalistic liberalism came to be seen as the natural state of human affairs obscured its own historical contingency. So persuasive were Rawls and Dworkin as abstract theorists that they made the power, prosperity, and security on

---

32 For an overview, see, for example, United Nations Association of Australia (UNAA), "The United Nations and the Rules-Based International Order" (Canberra: UNAA, 2015), https://www.unaa.org.au/wp-content/uploads/2015/07/UNAA_RulesBasedOrder_ARTweb3.pdf.

33 "Elections and Appointments, Election of the Human Rights Council," *General Assembly of the United Nations*, October 13, 2020, https://www.un.org/en/ga/75/meetings/elections/hrc.shtml.

34 Lorenzo Zucca, "Exit Hercules: Ronald Dworkin and the Crisis of the Age of Rights," in Salman Khurshid, Lokendra Malik, Veronica Rodriguez-Blanco eds., *Dignity In The Legal And Political Philosophy of Ronald Dworkin* (Oxford: Oxford University Press, 2018), 313–332; and Sir Stephen Laws, "There are substantial and unacceptable risks in moving to a legal constitution from our current political one," *LSE* Blog, September, 15, 2014.

35 See Annette Morris, "Spiralling or Stabilising? The Compensation Culture and Our Propensity to Claim Damages for Personal Injury," *Modern Law Review*, Vol. 70, No. 3 (2007), 349–378; and Joshua Rozenberg, "An insider's account of the Brenda agenda," *The Law Society Gazette*, February 3, 2020, https://www.lawgazette.co.uk/commentary-and-opinion/an-insiders-account-of-the-brenda-agenda/5102903.article.

36 Alan Ryan, "John Rawls" in Quentin Skinner, ed., *The Return of Grand Theory in the Human Sciences* (Cambridge: Cambridge University Press, 1985), 118; and Shami Chakrabarti, "On Liberty, Reading and Dissent" (Speech, London, November 30, 2015), The Reading Agency Lecture.

37 See Khurshid, Malik and Rodriguez-Blanco, *Dignity in the Legal and Political Philosophy of Ronald Dworkin*.

which the success of post-war liberalism depended seem irrelevant.[38] These were duly neglected in the decades after the Cold War, and by 2016 Western electorates had concluded that liberalism had 'lost much of its moral core and its centuries-long dedication to the public good.'[39] What it had also lost was any appreciation for its indebtedness to the practical idea that built the American prestige that had carried it across the globe.

In 1853 August Ludwig von Rochau, a liberal revolutionary and journalist in exile after the failed 1848 German revolution, published the first edition and volume of *Grundsätze der Realpolitik* (Foundations of Realpolitik). In it, he outlined four precepts to dispel naivety in the pursuit of liberal objectives under non-liberal conditions:

i. The law of the strong – power – is more decisive in politics than pure conscience or casuistry;
ii. Effective government requires the most powerful social forces to be harnessed and harmonized;
iii. Ideas matter, but widely and firmly held ideas matter more than those that are merely neat and worthy;
iv. The fast pace of modern politics means rulers must be attentive enough to public opinion and the zeitgeist to be able to overcome internal divisions with a sense of national pride and purpose.[40]

In short, moralism and utopianism would be the death of liberalism everywhere; pragmatism and purpose would realize it somewhere, albeit imperfectly and gradually. Rochau's realpolitik clearly contemplated a large space for idealism and conscientiousness in the practice of politics – it was neither immoral, amoral, chauvinistic, nor rankly Machiavellian.[41] Nevertheless, the original concept became distorted over time as it was co-opted by various people for various causes. Later German intellectuals jettisoned the liberal core of realpolitik and repurposed it as a vehicle for anti-Semitism and world domination, which the British then took for 'real realpolitik' and contrasted with their own honorable 'anti-realpolitik.'[42] While the traumatic experience of the Great War and Germany's defeat in it reinforced the British belief that

38 See generally Katrina Forrester, *In the Shadow of Justice: Postwar Liberalism and the Remaking of Political Philosophy* (Princeton: Princeton University Press, 2019).
39 Helena Rosenblatt, *The Lost History of Liberalism* (Princeton: Princeton University Press, 2018), 271
40 John Bew, *Realpolitik: A History* (Oxford: Oxford University Press, 2016), 32–35.
41 Ibid., 6.
42 Ibid., 85–86.

realpolitik was a vicious and self-defeating Prussian doctrine, its reception in the United States was altogether more enthusiastic.[43]

As early as 1915, the American reporter Walter Lippmann conceived of realpolitik as the exercise of rational self-interest in concert with other democratic powers in pursuit of liberal internationalism whose fruits would be global peace and prosperity.[44] Despite its association with the short-sighted British policy of appeasement and its perceived irrelevance to an isolationist America during the inter-war period, realpolitik re-emerged at the height of the Cold War as the United States sought to contain the Soviet Union.[45] The statesman with whom the term is most closely associated, Dr Henry Kissinger, was less of an amoral Machiavellian in the German fashion and more of an American idealist willing to make ruthless compromises in the short term to ensure the triumph of liberalism over communism in the long term.[46] Despite its successes – not least in playing China off against Russia – the heyday of Kissinger's brand of practical realpolitik was relatively short.

By the mid-1970s, the human and reputational costs associated with, for example, the Vietnam War and propping up various authoritarian regimes induced a 'New Anti-Realpolitik' movement under President Jimmy Carter (1977–1981).[47] This 'human rights crusade,' fed by the emerging legalistic liberalism of Rawls and Dworkin, introduced a novel 'moral factor' into foreign policy calculations: any course of action framed as detrimental to individual rights anywhere in the world could now have a direct impact on its efficacy both at home and abroad.[48] The credibility of realpolitik suffered a further blow once the Soviet Union collapsed – with the United States as the sole superpower left at the end of history, there seemed little need for something so compromised and gloomy.[49] For as long as the unipolar moment and faith in the rules-based international order held, minor non-liberal powers could be ostracized without much thought or overthrown in the name of emancipatory egalitarianism.[50] Now that the power of the Unites States has declined relative to that of China, however, and America's enemies have learned to weaponize the norms of the world order it created, the need for grand strategy has never been greater, and 'the timing for Realpolitik recovery could not be more opportune.'[51]

43   Ibid., 86–87, 114–122.
44   Ibid., 116.
45   Ibid., 123–183.
46   See generally Niall Ferguson, *Kissinger 1923–1968: The Idealist* (London: Penguin, 2016).
47   Bew, *Realpolitik*, 266–271.
48   Ibid., 271.
49   Ibid., 289.
50   Ibid., 290–295.
51   Frederico Seixas Dias, "From Realpolitik to realism: the American reception of a German conception of politics," *History of European Ideas*, Vol. 46, No. 4 (2020), 419.

The basic lesson here is that valuable ideas drift and degrade over time as they are misinterpreted, misrepresented, and misapplied. This is especially true of legal concepts, and it applies equally to institutions that have a reliable habit of forgetting their own history, purpose, and strength.[52] Set in historical context, then, the minting of 'lawfare' in late 2001 was more a synthesis than an invention. Its appearance at that time was neither a sign of cultural degeneration nor proof of geopolitical weakness – it was, whether Dunlap was conscious of it or not, the point of confluence of three great rivers of American thought: legal realism, liberal individualism, and practical realpolitik. Homegrown legal realism has helped generations of Americans to see the great worldly potential of law practiced well by good lawyers educated into 'good citizens and good men.'[53] Liberal individualism has spread American legal culture and institutions around the world while demonstrating the universal appeal of freedom, egalitarianism, and basic rights. Practical realpolitik is a monument to Americanization: a liberal German concept adapted to realize the destiny of the United States and deployed to overcome the greatest obstacles during the darkest times.

None of these traditions can sustain a doctrine of lawfare on its own, however. Interpreted narrowly and in isolation, legal realism presents a grim vision of law as a blunt instrument wielded by unscrupulous lawyers with no thought to anything beyond the case at hand.[54] Swallowed whole, liberal individualism becomes a straitjacket on statesmen, encouraging them to respond to geopolitical crises with hypocritical moralism or impulsive intervention where military force or careful diplomacy are required instead.[55] Left unchecked, a practical realpolitik that excuses any miserable compromise or expedient course of action will fast become an equally miserable substitute for principled sacrifice in the service of a liberal grand strategy.[56] Rather, the philosophical foundations of lawfare must be an admixture of all three working in combination: legal realism to ground and direct practice, tempered by liberal individualism to furnish moral vision, carried globally by realpolitik to maintain strategic

---

52 See David Ibbetson, "Milsom's Legal History," *Cambridge Law Journal*, Vol. 76, No. 2 (2017), 369–370; Francis O'Gorman, *Forgetfulness: Making the Modern Culture of Amnesia* (London: Bloomsbury, 2017); Adrian Goldsworthy, *The Fall of the West: The Death of the Roman Superpower* (London: Phoenix, 2010), 418–419, 423; and Christopher Andrew, *The Secret World: A History of Intelligence* (London: Allen Lane, 2018), 1.

53 Holmes, "The Path of the Law," 335.

54 See generally Martha C. Nussbaum, "Why Practice Needs Ethical Theory: Particularism, Principle, and Bad Behavior," in *Moral Particularism*, Brad Hooker & Margaret Olivia Little, eds. (Oxford: Clarendon Press, 2000), 50–86.

55 See Henry Kissinger, "The Limits of Universalism" (Speech, New York City, April 26, 2012), Edmund Burke Award for Service to Culture and Society, https://www.henryakissinger.com/speeches/the-limits-of-universalism.

56 For an unfair but illustrative example of this type of accusation, see Christopher Hitchens, *The Trial of Henry Kissinger* (London: Atlantic, 2014).

competitiveness. Yet if it is to be of any practical utility to the United States and its allies, lawfare must escape the abstract realm and return to earth on the back of doctrine.

3.2 The Doctrine of Total Lawfare

Simply *redefining* lawfare yet again will achieve nothing. Rather, it must be radically reconceptualized as a viable *doctrine* that is at once straightforward, futureproof, commodious to myriad forms, and applicable with precision to every relevant dimension of contemporary geopolitics.

To this end, the authors propose a turn to 'total lawfare' delineated as follows:

> The strategic and systematic creation or use of law (international or domestic) by a geopolitical actor (state or non-state) to further (directly or indirectly) a geopolitical objective (offensive, defensive or reconstitutive) against an (actual or anticipated) adversary and any of their (identifiable or potential) assets.

Each aspect of this requires careful elaboration to demonstrate its analytical and operational utility.

3.2.1 Theoretical Components

To mirror the opening sentiment of General Erich Ludendorff's (1865–1937) *Der totale Krieg* (1935), the present authors abhor elaborate theory and do not intend to write a comprehensive philosophical tract on legal warfare. What follows is merely a brusque proclamation of the distinguishing conceptual features and ethical limits of total lawfare.

The classic Western distinction between 'limited' and 'absolute' war was first drawn by Carl von Clausewitz in his canonical *On War* (1832). Put crudely, limited wars were fought between the rulers of early modern states with 'war machines distinct and separate from the rest of society' with the aim of wringing territorial, financial, or political concessions from their defeated opponent. Such conflicts were ultimately about limited self-interest and generally settled by decisive engagements on the battlefield, which meant that the violence was contained to begin with and tended to fade away as each side ran out of resources. By contrast, absolute wars emerged after the French Revolution injected ideological fervor into warfighting and made it the 'business of the people' themselves, implicating the entire citizenry in death struggles between nations 'untrammeled by any conventional constraints.'[57] In Clausewitz's pre-industrial era, absolute war was an unattainable Platonic ideal for belligerent nations and his conception of it remained fundamentally instrumental (i.e. it was the logical escalation of violence intended to force a decisive battle to attain particular policy objectives).[58]

As Ludendorff himself grasped, the Clausewitzian concept of absolute war was therefore too limited and limiting past the arrival of totalitarian ideology and modern material conditions in the early 20th century. It simply could not convey the metaphysical and civilizational stakes of modern conflict in the aftermath of the Russian Revolution, as entire blocs of advanced nations lined up to confront one another over the very nature and direction of humanity itself.[59] While some scholars have dismissed Ludendorff's ideas as 'neither original nor interesting,' *Der totale Krieg* contributes far more to Western strategic thought than a mere catchphrase.[60] In it, Ludendorff goes further than any previous military theorist by arguing that every national resource – military and civilian, material and intellectual – be harnessed and mobilized against every resource the enemy possessed.[61] The point was not to engineer the most favorable conditions under which to fight a decisive battle; it was to create a comprehensive process capable of generating a comprehensive victory.[62]

While the subsequent experience of the 20th century has understandably made anything smacking of 'total' unpalatable to the Western mind, Ludendorff's concept – more than any other – best captures the essence of the new cold war with China: the stakes are civilizational, the motivations ideological, the arenas multifarious, the resources required immense, the military/civilian distinction meaningless, and the law a connecting thread throughout. This reality renders even the best classical lawfare literature obsolete: confronting the PRC with a 'limited' lawfare strategy tied to rudimentary state capabilities, military operations, and international law is unlikely to succeed given the scale and sophistication of Chinese lawfare. However, turning lawfare total is ostensibly a hard sell given that 'total' conjures up grim images of collective punishment, limitless violence, and thoroughgoing

---

57 See Michael Howard, *Clausewitz* (Oxford, 2002), 50–51.

58 Jan Willem Honig, "The Idea of Total War: From Clausewitz to Ludendorff," in *Pacific War as Total War: Proceedings of the 2011 International Forum on War History* (Tokyo: National Institute for Defence Studies, September 14, 2012), 31–33.

59 See Arthur Herman, *1917: Lenin, Wilson, and the Birth of the New World Disorder* (Harper Perennial, 2018).

60 Roger Chickering, "Sore Loser: Ludendorff's Total War," in Roger Chickering and Stig Förster, eds, *The Shadows of Total War: Europe, East Asia, and the United States, 1919–1939* (New York: Cambridge University Press, 2003), 176–177.

61 Chickering, "Sore Loser," 177–178; Jan Willem Honig, "The Idea of Total War: From Clausewitz to Ludendorff," in *Pacific War as Total War: Proceedings of the 2011 International Forum on War History* (Tokyo: National Institute for Defence Studies, September 14, 2012), 30, 36.

62 Honig, "The Idea of Total War," 31–33, 40–41.

authoritarianism. If it is not to result in such horrors, and if the West is not to emulate the PRC by cutting a swathe through constitutional principle or choking free society with militarized regulation, the doctrine must be carefully framed.

The liberal conscience, as Michael Howard famously observed, is typically appalled by conflict.[63] That lawfare has effectively become the 'sole province' of the enemies of the Western powers is due in no small part to this deep-rooted squeamishness.[64] Even while Russia and China forge ahead with already sophisticated lawfare programs, the West is 'barely fighting back,' as many of its most eminent jurists obstinately refuse to entertain the merest instrumentalization of law in response.[65] Articles warning of 'invocations of colonial discourses of non-Western legal [belligerence],' the 'securitization of human rights,' and the dangers of 'legal mobilization' abound.[66] These qualms are understandable, laudable even, but dangerously overblown. Despite the terminology employed, total lawfare need not be indiscriminate or unrestricted – there are practical and ethical limits to its scope and use both by and within the West.

The practical issues can be dispatched swiftly. First, while waging lawfare may be less costly in terms of blood and treasure than fighting a kinetic war, the former will never fully supersede the latter for as long as human nature remains what it is and the incentives – political, religious, material – exist for societies to compete with one another.[67] By the same token, law cannot and should not supplant politics as the primary means by which democratic nations make difficult but legitimate decisions.[68] Placing excessive faith in technocratic lawcraft when statesmanship and generalship are required will only frustrate good governance at home and effective leadership in the field.[69] Law's empire may be expanding, but it must never become all-consuming. Nevertheless, wherever law does have a place, it should be designed and practiced as well as is humanly possible, a self-evident imperative that imposes certain methodological constraints. The danger, in other words, is that total

63 See Michael Howard, *War and the Liberal Conscience* (London: Temple Smith, 1978).
64 Goldenziel, "Law as a Battlefield," 1096.
65 Kittrie, *Lawfare*, 33–35; and Goldenziel, "Law as a Battlefield," 1089–1090.
66 Freya Irani, "'Lawfare', US military discourse, and the colonial constitution of law and war," *European Journal of International Security*, Vol. 3, No. 1 (2018), 113–133; Neve Gordon, "Human Rights as a Security Threat: Lawfare and the Campaign against Human Rights NGOs," *Law & Society Review*, Vol. 48, No. 2 (2014) 311–344; Thandiwe Matthews, "Interrogating the Debates Around Lawfare and Legal Mobilization: A Literature Review," *Journal of Human Rights Practice*, Vol. 15, No. 1 (2023), 24–45.
67 Goldenziel, "Law as a Battlefield," 1101; and Kittrie, *Lawfare*, 3.
68 See Jonathan Sumption, *Trials of the State: Law and the Decline of Politics* (London: Profile, 2019).
69 Nigel Biggar, *What's Wrong with Rights?* chaps. 10 and 12.

lawfare done badly at scale brings on 'the polar night of icy darkness' to engulf our heavily bureaucratic and increasingly stagnant political culture.[70]

To escape this 'iron cage,' therefore, any nascent Western lawfare programs should be informed by the method of juridification and the Tacitean insights of nudge theory. The former is simply a technique of translating broad culture war controversies into solvable legal equations; the latter is simply a way of designing laws that are surgically precise, intuitive, and require minimal enforcement.[71] The basic point is that technical reforms must precisely address well-defined problems in a proportionate manner. For total lawfare to be waged effectively, however, it has still to be as ethical as it is efficient – an efficient but seemingly amoral or immoral lawfare strategy will be self-defeating as regards reputation and legitimacy. It is of categorical importance, therefore, that Western powers do not engage in what Kittrie calls 'illicit lawfare.'[72] This effectively means that if they are to uphold the rule of law, they cannot, for example, pass legislation that overrides their constitutional commitments to human rights and equality, or condone litigation tactics that breach their own evidentiary procedures and professional ethics. Such principles distinguish the West from its adversaries, and uncompromising adherence to them is especially important in relation to target acquisition.

At a time when racial tensions run high across the Anglosphere, it is worth noting that the English language is 'notoriously poor' at denoting collective phenomena.[73] This is a major handicap when it comes to analyzing any problem with a group dimension, including lawfare against state and non-state adversaries. Fortunately, the remedy can be found in the work of another German genius, the jurist Otto von Gierke (1841–1921). An ardent militarist who described his own experience of war as 'an hour of consecration,' he nevertheless achieved considerable international and cross-partisan popularity at the turn of the 20th century as the originator of political pluralism.[74] His disciples included Oakeshott and no less a figure than Oliver Wendell Holmes

---

70 Max Weber quoted in Peter Lassman and Ronald Spiers, eds., *Weber: Political Writings* (Cambridge: Cambridge University Press, 1994), xvi; Niall Ferguson, *The Great Degeneration: How Institutions Decay and Economies Die* (London: Penguin, 2014); and David Graeber, *The Utopia of Rules: On Technology, Stupidity, and the Secret Joys of Bureaucracy* (London: Melville House, 2015).

71 Karen Knop, Ralf Michaels, and Annelise Riles, "From Multiculturalism to Technique: Feminism, Culture, and the Conflict of Laws Style," *Stanford Law Review*, Vol. 64 (2012), 589–656; and David Halpern, *Inside the Nudge Unit: How Small Changes Can Make a Big Difference* (London: Penguin, 2016).

72 Kittrie, *Lawfare*, 8.

73 Antony Black, ed., "Introduction," in Otto von Gierke, *Community in Historical Perspective: A Translation of Selections from Das deutsche Genossenschaftsrecht*, trans. Mary Fischer (Cambridge: Cambridge University Press, 1990), xxxiii.

74 Quoted in Andrew Sparkes, *Talking Politics: A Wordbook* (London: Routledge, 1994), 97.

himself, whose most famous dissent was heavily influenced by Gierke's ideas on corporate personality.[75]

Gierke also produced what remains the clearest typology of collective entities available, through his translators, in English. According to him, the nation as a whole was akin to a living organism and ecosystem of groups all enmeshed in the sinews of law. Those necessary to the health of society were: the state as the only body with a 'plenitude of powers' to represent and govern the whole of society; the family as 'the securest foundation of our society'; and the fellowship as any legitimate civil society enterprise 'with body and members and a will of its own.'[76] However, he specified two other forms of group that were harmful both to the others and to the nation itself: (1) the vassal institution (*Anstalt*) and (2) the privileged institution (*priviligierte Korporation*). The former, which might include government departments and state-funded non-government organizations, were mere instruments of a superior religious or state power with no intrinsic autonomy; the latter, which might equally include monopolistic corporations and self-interested trade unions, were degenerate fellowships oblivious to the common good and concerned only with their own wealth, status, and legal privileges. Though they might bear a superficial resemblance, these could not be regarded as true fellowships deserving of legal protection, and it was incumbent on the state to prevent them from forming and to cull them when they did.[77] This greatly simplified typology is indispensable to modern lawfare. First, it precludes any notion of collective punishment based on class or race or religion, as these categories are not meaningful entities with agency.[78] Accordingly, total lawfare can never be used to justify attacks on, for example, 'Chinese people' or 'Asians.' Second, it clarifies the real and legitimate targets in general terms:

(a) Not 'all of China' but the PRC, meaning the assets – human and institutional, material and intellectual – under the direction of, and/or actually or potentially available to, the CCP which currently controls the Chinese state;

(b) Not 'every Chinese person' but anyone or any organization working, directly or indirectly, intentionally or unintentionally, to advance the aims and interests of the CCP.

---

75 Ewan McGaughey, '"Introduction" to Otto von Gierke, "The Social Role of Private Law" *German Law Journal*, Vol. 19, No. 4 (2018), 1021; and Luke O'Sullivan, "Michael Oakeshott on European Political History," *History of Political Thought*, Vol. 21, No. 1 (2000), 132–151.

76 John D. Lewis, *The Genossenschaft Theory of Otto Von Gierke: A Study in Political Thought* (Madison: University of Wisconsin, 2013), 61–65.

77 Ibid., 60, fn 21; Gierke, *Community in Historical Perspective*, 105–106.

78 Otto Von Gierke, "The Nature of Human Associations" in Lewis, *Genossenschaft Theory of Otto Von Gierke*, 151.

3.2.2 Practical Components

Translating the theory of total lawfare into practice requires three things: (1) institutionalization; (2) geopolitical objectives; and (3) a whole-of-society approach. Each shall be discussed in turn.

3.2.2.1 Institutionalization

Total lawfare is not so 'infinitely plastic' as to be indistinguishable from mundane law-making and litigation.[79] Rather, it is driven by strategic intent and institutionalized in a systematic manner, which means creating or using law – broadly understood to include any domestic or international legal instrument, authority, norm, or theory – for geopolitical purposes in a way that is deliberate and programmatic rather than incidental and ad hoc. For any of this to occur, lawfare must first be institutionalized within and beyond the state. While Western powers possess vast cybersecurity agencies – such as the NSA in the US and GCHQ in the UK – they are yet to create anything comparable in the domain of lawfare. In the US context, Goldenziel's proposed 'lawfare office' would be a model of good practice, combining as it does research, operational, and educational functions while interfacing with existing government agencies.[80] Similarly, in the UK context, it would be better to remove responsibility for lawfare from the Ministry of Justice and create instead dedicated sections within each ministry overseen by a dedicated lawfare agency to complement, and coordinate with, the established security agencies.

Raising such institutions from scratch will require tremendous political will and sustained financial investment; these may not always, or may never, be forthcoming from the central government. This opens up space for private enterprises to create a next-generation defense industry and specialized training courses, as well as opportunities for NGOs and civic-minded philanthropists to invest in civilian-led campaigns in defense of their nation, just as the Roman elite once did to raise a fleet in their death-struggle with Carthage during the First Punic War.[81] Such organizations may wage lawfare in their own right – albeit subject to regulation by the host state – while also entering into hybrid arrangements with the government whereby they are contracted to perform specific tasks or serve in an advisory capacity to state-led operations.[82] Such lawfare may proceed in an open and direct manner – such as using government

---

79 Eric Loeffeld, "The World Revolutionary Origins of the Crime of Aggression: Sovereignty, (Anti-) Imperialism, and the Soviet Union's Contradictory Geopolitics of Global Justice," *Harvard Journal of the Legal Left*, Vol. 12, No. 1 (2019), 29; and Goldenziel, "Law as a Battlefield," 1098.
80 Goldenziel, "Law as a Battlefield," 1161–1170.
81 Adrian Goldsworthy, *The Fall of Carthage* (London: Phoenix, 2006), 123.
82 Kittrie, *Lawfare*, 106–107.

lawyers to litigate or defend against adversaries in a specific legal action – or they may be clandestine and indirect – such as discreetly funding a particular party against an adversary in strategically important litigation seemingly unconnected to the donor's immediate activities or interests.[83] As lawfare becomes more institutionalized and public–private partnerships more common, there is every reason to expect a tradition of practice to build throughout the West as expertise, tactics, and information are shared, mistakes learned from, and victories exploited for maximum effect. Thus, while the state will remain the most important driver of total lawfare given its inherent geopolitical character, it need not and should not be the only actor involved in waging it against state and non-state adversaries.

3.2.2.2 Geopolitical Objectives

The scope of total lawfare must encompass broad geopolitical objectives as well as strictly military ones. These may be offensive, designed to actively inflict damage on an adversary. This would include attempts by the US to impose financial sanctions on Iran to halt its nuclear program without bombing it, private domestic litigation to seize Cuban and Iranian assets as compensation for terrorist activities, and NGOs litigating against multinational companies to name and shame them for trading in breach of sanctions against Iran.[84] The objectives may be defensive, designed to deflect or mitigate an adversary's offensive operations. This would include the UK's attempts to defend against vexatious human rights claims brought by Islamists to inflict reputational damage on the state, the legal maneuverings of the US and its allies to frustrate China's expansionist maritime claims in the South China Sea, and the longstanding US policy of opposing participation in the ICC to reduce its exposure to lawfare.[85]

Geopolitical objectives may also be reconstitutive, designed to internally reorder one's society so that it can flourish better under inclement geopolitical conditions. Reconstitutive measures are not merely mundane and idealistic attempts to make society a better place or settle peaceful domestic disputes between constituent parts of a nation and/or rival political parties (such as between the Scottish National Party and the UK government). Rather, they are policies implemented in the knowledge that one's state exists in relation to, and in tension with, competing geopolitical actors. The point is to use law to

---

83 For a range of examples of the former, see Kittrie, *Lawfare*, 103–109; and for an unconventional and brilliant example of the latter, see Ryan Holiday, *Conspiracy: A True Story of Power, Sex, and a Billionaire's Secret Plot to Destroy a Media Empire* (London: Profile Books, 2018).

84 Kittrie, *Lawfare*, 16–17, 111.

85 Kittrie, *Lawfare*, 2, 29, 165–168; and Overseas Operations (Service Personnel and Veterans) Act 2021, c.23 (Eng.).

build 'legal resilience' – or, ideally, legal 'antifragility'[86] – so that the critical institutions and infrastructure of society are rendered more resilient against threats while the rule of law is itself strengthened 'against violations and subversion of its norms, institutions and processes.'[87] This will typically involve 'shaping the environment' strategies to reconstitute aspects of the domestic legal system to make it harder for adversaries and their agents to exploit the opportunities for mischief inherent in any open, democratic, globalized society.[88] The need for such reconstitutive measures is highlighted in two major new studies of Chinese aggression which conclude that the West's greatest vulnerability at present is the perception – ceaselessly exploited and amplified by Beijing and Moscow – that its leading nations are in internal disarray and global decline.[89] This gives the CCP 'far greater room to deploy its soft and sharp power tools' and, if it is to be discredited, requires a robust reconstitutive program to shore up democracy at home and broadcast its success and appeal abroad.[90]

Any and all of these objectives may be pursued regardless of whether or not hostilities are openly declared, and whether or not the adversary is an actual enemy or an anticipated threat against which it is best to guard in advance. They may apply directly to the adversarial entity (e.g. the PRC or Jihadist network) or indirectly against its resources including identifiable agents and assets (financial, reputational, cultural, and so forth), proxy institutions or companies under its control (e.g. Huawei and state-owned enterprises), vassal states which may or may not be an adversary in their own right (e.g. Belarus as Russia's junior partner), or diaspora community networks that could enable power to be projected from abroad into the jurisdiction (e.g. transnational clans acting as foreign policy instruments of Pakistan in UK politics).[91] Such a variegated approach is necessary to account for the kaleidoscopic nature of postmodern geopolitical conflict in which certainty and convention have given way to information warfare and hybrid operations.

3.2.2.3 Whole-of-Society Approach

In combination with conventional military and diplomatic efforts, the doctrine of total lawfare will be essential to defeating, in detail, enemy lawfare campaigns.

86 Meaning a system that is 'beyond resilience and robustness' in that it grows and benefits from shocks, stressors, and volatility – see Nassim Nicholas Taleb, *Anti-Fragile: Things that Gain from Disorder* (London: Penguin, 2013), 3.

87 Aurel Sari, "Legal Resilience in an Era of Grey Zone Conflicts and Hybrid Threats," *Cambridge Review of International Affairs* Vol. 33, No. 6 (2019), 846–867.

88 Goldenziel, "Law as a Battlefield," 1097.

89 Walton, *Spies*, 514–515; Kurlantzick, *Beijing's Global Media Offensive*, 366–367.

90 Ibid.

91 See Nash, *British Islam and English Law*, chaps. 7 and 8.

While each Western nation will require its own particular strategy, which Kittrie and Goldenziel have already outlined in admirable detail for the US, it is worth noting a few specific examples and proposals to illustrate the range of legal countermeasures required in relation to Chinese unrestricted lawfare.

To repel technology acquisition operations, prudent next steps to protect sensitive data and technology would include: designating Pakistan – both in its own right and on account of its close economic and military partnership with China – as a 'country of concern' for the purposes of the CHIPS and Science Act 2022, improving Western coordination on technology export-control enforcement, and intensifying the US-led effort to blacklist Chinese-owned companies and drive them from sensitive sectors. Meanwhile, the UK's National Security and Investment Act 2021 should be strengthened (given the government's reluctance to intervene in the NWF purchase) by introducing a rebuttable presumption against any foreign direct investment in sensitive sectors.[92] More aggressive investigations of Western tech companies operating labs in China (under its MCF laws) and publicly shaming them for such 'seemingly treasonous' behavior will be essential to mitigating industrial espionage, as would prohibiting Western universities on pain of sanction from accepting Chinese investment and students in sensitive fields relevant to national security.[93]

As for countering attempts at power projection, the Western powers need to coordinate and improve their preparedness for PRC-instigated massed lawfare attacks within their domestic jurisdictions as well as across international fora by anticipating likely tactics, all while maximizing US preeminence in treaty creation for current and new arenas of geopolitical competition (such as space and cyberspace).[94] They would also need to litigate more aggressively themselves, and support proxies directly or indirectly, at international law to rebut and ridicule PRC territorial claims, all while noisily shaming the CCP's corruption of international institutions and its violations of human rights, climate accords, and international treaties.[95] While partly defensive and a signal

---

92 "US Blacklists seven Chinese supercomputer groups," *BBC News*, April 9, 2021, https://www.bbc.co.uk/news/business-56685136; Alex Fang, "Bowing to US pressure, Chinese owner sells gay dating app Grindr," *Nikkei Asia*, March 7, 2020, https://asia.nikkei.com/Business/Business-deals/Bowing-to-US-pressure-Chinese-owner-sells-gay-dating-app-Grindr; Sion Barry, "Why hasn't the Competition and Markets Authority reviewed the Chinese takeover of Newport Wafer Fab, *BusinessLive*, November 1, 2021, https://www.business-live.co.uk/opinion-analysis/hasnt-competition-markets-authority-reviewed-22026852.

93 Eric Lutz, "Peter Thiel Accuses Google of 'Treasonous' relationship with China," *Vanity Fair*, July 15, 2019, https://www.vanityfair.com/news/2019/07/peter-thiel-accuses-google-of-treasonous-relationship-with-china; and Radomir Tylecote and Robert Clark, *Inadvertently Arming China? The Chinese military complex and its potential exploitation of scientific research at UK universities* (Civitas, February 2021).

94 Kittire, *Lawfare*, 191–195.

95 Ibid.; and Goldenziel, "Law as a Battlefield," 1156–1172.

to the international community of nations, such efforts should be conducted in an offensive spirit with a view to influencing – so far as is possible – Chinese public opinion against the CCP's corruption given the premium placed upon law-abidingness within that culture.[96]

As regards counter-subversion, Western security agencies which 'no longer undertake counter-subversion work' should be put on high alert and ordered to resume it right away.[97] Reforming the reverse burden of proof in English defamation law – notorious the world over for its amenability to libel tourism and strategic lawsuits against public participation (SLAPPs) – would neutralize a major Western handicap by facilitating more aggressive reporting on Chinese front groups.[98] Modernizing treason and official secrets laws to encompass espionage and infiltration attempts to aid undeclared enemies during formal peacetime should also be made a priority.[99] Globally, pressure should be applied to the PRC's own reputation by, for example, promoting and supporting independent organizations such as the Uyghur Tribunal (UT), recently formed in the UK 'to investigate China's alleged Genocide and crimes against Humanity against Uyghur, Kazakh and other Turkic Muslim populations.'[100] Such bodies are a major irritant to the CCP, which angrily denounces the UT as 'a pseudo court with no legal basis or authority whatsoever' and 'an anti-China farce based entirely on lies and disinformation. It is a front for political manipulation by certain anti-China elements to smear China, mislead the British public and disrupt China-UK relations.'[101]

The West has much to learn from its allies on the frontline of authoritarian aggression. Notably, Taiwan's 'whole-of-society approach' to Chinese political warfare which incorporates 'factchecking by civil society organizations, government-sponsored education for media literacy, a technology sector that actively curbed inauthentic behavior online ... [plus robust] "fake news"

96 Goldenziel, "Law as a Battlefield," 1158–1161.

97 "What we do," *The Security Service (MI5)*, accessed October 23, 2023, https://www.mi5.gov .uk/what-we-do.

98 See generally Nick Cohen, *You Can't Read This Book: Censorship in an Age of Freedom* (New York: Harper Collins, 2013).

99 For the UK context, see Richard Ekins et al., Aiding the Enemy (Policy Exchange, July 25, 2018), https://policyexchange.org.uk/publication/aiding-the-enemy; and Dan Sabbagh, "Why prosecutors are reluctant to use 'notoriously flaky' Official Secrets Act," *The Guardian*, September 13, 2023. https://www.theguardian.com/law/2023/sep/13/why-prosecutors-reluctant-to -use-notoriously-flaky-official-secrets-act.

100 *Uyghur Tribunal*, accessed November 16, 2021, https://uyghurtribunal.com.

101 "Embassy Spokesperson's Remarks on So-called 'Second Hearing' of 'Uyghur tribunal,'" Embassy of the People's Republic of China in the United Kingdom of Great Britain and Northern Ireland, September 14, 2021, https://www.mfa.gov.cn/ce/ceuk//eng/PressandMedia /Spokepersons/t1906888.htm.

regulations, and legislation criminalizing foreign election interference.'[102] Ukraine's experience is similarly instructive, for its own whole-of-society approach 'pressed its corporations into service in the legal war' against Russia by encouraging them to file international arbitration and asset seizure lawsuits against Russian proxies.[103] A good start for NATO would be an international effort to establish a full-time translation program for major PRC lawfare texts, given that all of the relevant books are unavailable to the majority of Western scholars lacking fluency in the Chinese language.[104] Relatedly, the financial and career incentives for legal academics and law schools should be rebalanced to ensure that Western international law expertise is not unduly confined to certain traditional fields (notably human rights and the law of war) but rather extends, rapidly and at scale, to cover every subfield being prioritized by the CCP.[105] Further to this, it would be advisable to re-found the Cold-War era Active Measures Working Group to directly confront and 'respond comprehensively and give importance to the problem of disinformation – that is, to define it, to create institutions to tackle it and to draw attention to it at the highest level.'[106]

A whole-of-society approach to total lawfare would be a proportionate addition to the West's geopolitical arsenal regardless of whether or not the anticipated conflict is limited to containable territorial spats (e.g. between the UK and Argentina over the Falkland Islands) or constitutes an all-out and indefinite civilizational struggle (e.g. the West against the CCP and/or Islamism). This is chiefly because modern hybrid threats cannot be compartmentalized and Western powers must now be prepared to confront everything, everywhere, all at once with an integrated strategy. While there is some recognition of this in British defense strategy given the recurrent emphasis on a 'whole-of-government approach' to national security, this is more restrictive than a whole-of-society doctrine which marshals all relevant non-government organizations and the entire private sector against the enemy.[107] In short and in general, then, the best response to Chinese unrestricted lawfare is total

---

102 Sean Quirk, "Lawfare in the Disinformation Age: Chinese Interference in Taiwan's 2020 Elections," *Harvard International Law Journal*, Vol. 62 No. 2 (2021), 525, 559.

103 Goldenziel, "An Alternative to Zombieing," 12–13.

104 Kittrie, *Lawfare*, 10.

105 Roberts, *Is International Law International?*, 226–230.

106 Nicholas J. Cull, Vasily Gatov, Peter Pomerantsev, Anne Applebaum, and Alistair Shawcross, "Soviet Subversion, Disinformation and Propaganda: How the West Fought Against it – An Analytic History, with Lessons for the Present – Final Report" (London: LSE Consulting, October 2017), 26. https://www.lse.ac.uk/business/consulting/reports/soviet-subversion-disinformation-and-propaganda-how-the-west-fought-against-it.

107 *Strategic Trends Programme Future Operating Environment 2035*, 1st ed. (Ministry of Defence, 2014), 5, https://assets.publishing.service.gov.uk/government/uploads/system/uploads/attachment_data/file/1076877/FOE.pdf; *Strategic Operating Concept 2025*, 16.

lawfare, and in that regard the West has a great deal to do if it is ever to counter, let alone defeat, the PRC in this geopolitical domain.

3.3 The Endgame of the Beginning: New Defense

The historical record is replete with societies that, for one reason or another,
were unable or unwilling to adopt emerging technologies with great strategic
potential.[108] Whether the Greco-Roman taboo against human cadaveric
dissection for medical research, or the Ottoman refusal to adopt the printing
press and modern financial instruments, or the Qing Empire's sluggishness
as regards deep-water navies, fortress design, and autonomous institutions,
or Revolutionary France's reluctance to adopt the British-invented carronade
for sea combat, or the British dismissal of submersibles as an 'underhand
method of attack' just prior to the Great War, nations across the world have
proven themselves time and again, and always at great cost to themselves
and their people, either too proud or too blinkered to embrace unconventional
innovations.[109] This is the same trap that the contemporary West has fallen
into with lawfare – a combination of willful neglect and sneering dismissal of
the adversaries using to ever greater effect.

For better and for worse, conflict has been a formative influence on humanity since time immemorial and has bequeathed us with so much of all that
civilization has to offer, from engineering to economics to ethics.[110] Waging
total lawfare does not mean that Western powers have to become like their
enemies in every respect by abandoning their commitment to non-instrumental rules, or transform themselves into pure Oakeshottian enterprise associations dedicated to nothing but geopolitical conflict. It does, however, require
them first to admit that their enemies currently possess a better understanding
of, and capabilities for (ab)using, our unique legal heritage which should be

---

108 For a fascinating overview of the West's tortured historical relationship with unconventional
weaponry and tactics, see Adrienne Mayor, *Greek Fire, Poison Arrows & Scorpion Bombs:
Biological and Chemical Weapons in the Ancient World* (London: Overlook-Duckworth, 2003).

109 See, respectively, Sanjib Kumar Ghosh, "Human cadaveric dissection: a historical account
from ancient Greece to the modern era," *Anatomy of Cell Biology*, Vol. 48, No. 3 (2015),
153–169; Bernard Lewis, *The Muslim Discovery of Europe* (London: Phoenix, 2000), 168; and
Timur Kuran, *The Long Divergence: How Islamic Law Held Back the Middle East* (Princeton:
Princeton University Press, 2011); Tonio Andrade, *The Gunpowder Age: China, Military Innovation and the Rise of the West in World History* (Princeton: Princeton University Press, 2016),
299–302; Nicolas M, "Napoléon et l'évolution de l'artillerie des vaisseaux," [Napoleon and the
evolution of ship artillery], *Trois-Ponts!* December 10, 2013, https://troisponts.net/2013/12/10/
napoleon-et-levolution-de-lartillerie-des-vaisseaux; and Richard Connaughton, *Rising Sun and
Tumbling Bear: Russia's War with Japan* (London: Cassell, 2003), 62.

110 See Ian Morris, *War: What Is It Good For? The Role of Conflict in Civilisation from Primates
to Robots* (London: Profile, 2014); and Margaret MacMillan, *War: How Conflict Shaped Us*
(London: Profile, 2020).

being used better and for better ends.[111] This admission must lead in turn to an acknowledgment that the West has an intellectual tradition every bit as rich as those of its enemies from which to synthesize an effective and principled total lawfare strategy. Across the Anglophone world, at least, a reacquaintance with American legal realism, realpolitik, and liberalism is therefore essential for the intellectual legitimization of total lawfare and its eventual integration into geopolitical grand strategy in coordination with allies. In short, total lawfare needs to become, and be understood as being, a natural extension of the West's politico-legal traditions.

It must also be rendered legible to private enterprise and public-private research-financing systems such as DARPA and In-Q-Tel if it is to benefit from adequate investment and rapid innovation. Fortunately, Peter Thiel has already outlined the issues, supplied the vernacular, and created flourishing precedents in the 'New Defense' industry:

> Technology entrepreneurs and investors would do well to return to hard and important problems. As globalization proceeds apace, the decisive unsolved problem concerns the issue of security. There remains a tremendous need for real defense against the proliferation of destructive technologies – reaching well beyond the Orwellian 'defense' industry, with its proclivity for constructing new contraptions that kill large numbers of people. Along with the New Economy and New Media, there should exist a valuable sector that could be described as New Defense – at least in any twenty-first century in which humanity does not blow itself up. The absence of such a sector serves as a subtle reminder of the complacent myopia of Silicon Valley venture capitalists investing in 'technology.'[112]

As part of his optimistic vision for averting a 'secular apocalypse,' Thiel founded multiple thriving defense companies within the last two decades including Palantir Technologies (data analytics for the intelligence and finances sectors) and Anduril Industries (autonomous systems with military applications). With a market capitalization of $32 billion and $8.5 billion, respectively, in 2023, the rapid success of these companies suggests that there is a large market gap and ample demand for an advanced total lawfare industry driven by new model lawfare firms. Creating this new branch of New Defense may be only the endgame of the beginning of the long game against

---

111 On this point see Richard Mullender, "Lawfare and the international human rights movement," in Rob Dickinson et al., eds., *Examining Critical Perspectives on Human Rights* (Cambridge University Press, 2012), 274–278.

112 Peter Thiel, "The Optimistic Thought Experiment," *Hoover Institution*, January 29, 2008, https://www.hoover.org/research/optimistic-thought-experiment.

the PRC, but without it the West will struggle to stay in the game at all, let alone play to win.

3.4 General Conclusion

The preceding parts of this book illustrated that Western powers have gifted China a long and widening lead in the field of lawfare. This stems from the absence of serious jurisprudential apologia among the former and the inheritance of legal instrumentalism by the latter.[113] Having redressed that deficiency, the book proceeded to translate relevant theories and definitions into a doctrine of total lawfare for use by Western powers against any adversary. Institutionalized and operationalized properly, this doctrine will be more than a match for Chinese unrestricted warfare, and 'the United States seems far better suited to be a lawfare superpower' if only it would take to the field with conviction.[114] What is more, that field remains heavily skewed in the West's favor given the overwhelming global dominance of, and preference for, the English-language, common law approaches, and Western practitioners in international legal disputes.[115] The future of warfare will be dominated, more than ever before, by high-technology and highly-skilled specialists rather than massed manpower and brute force alone.[116] As much was acknowledged in the UK's 2021 *Integrated Review of Security, Defence, Development and Foreign Policy*:

> [S]ystemic competition will further test the line between peace and war, as malign actors use a wider range of tools – such as economic statecraft, cyber-attacks, disinformation and proxies – to achieve their objectives without open confrontation or conflict. The UK is likely to remain a priority target for such threats. Our ability to deter aggression will be challenged by new techniques and technologies.[117]

To compete under these conditions and emerge victorious in the conflicts to come, the West must marry the 'cathedral thinking' of the visionary statesman – grand strategy on a global, centuries-long scale – with the low tactical

---

113 On this point compare Dunlap, "Does lawfare need an apologia?" 121–143; and Cheng, *Winning Without Fighting*, 6.
114 Kittire, *Lawfare*, 161.
115 Roberts, *Is International Law International?*, 254–275.
116 See generally Lawrence Freedman, *The Future of War: A History* (London: Penguin, 2018), pt 3.
117 U.K. Cabinet Office, *Global Britain in a competitive age*, 28.

cunning of the trial lawyer.[118] This requires no starry-eyedness about the rules-based international order or an unconditional love of American leadership, merely an acknowledgment that a Western-led world is better than one led by dragons and their snakish clients.[119] Indeed, such a world would be worse in every conceivable way – environmentally, economically, politically, humanely – and Chinese unrestricted lawfare is bringing it closer every day.[120] In broad terms, this necessitates a recognition by Western powers that America's unipolar moment has subsided into a new era of great power rivalry which must be countered with a proactive grand strategy: building an 'empire of trust' with traditional allies and new partners in the developing world (albeit via targeted investment and conditional aid)[121] to deny Chinese ambitions while wearing down their endeavors at every opportunity, everywhere, without triggering a direct kinetic confrontation.[122] Rather than wasting blood and treasure on futile attempts at democracy-building across the Islamic world, counter-terror and counter-insurgency operations must be conducted with unprecedented ruthlessness to neutralize threats and constrain Chinese maneuvers.[123]

The PRC has been playing a canny long game against Western interests for decades, and it is high time that the United States responds in kind to bring about the eventual collapse of the CCP.[124] To this end, the Western allies will need to engage in joined-up thinking about defense to obtain and exploit better intelligence about carefully concealed weaknesses as well as the relationship between internal discord and China's international behavior.[125] This is where total lawfare fits in – to neutralize the CCP aggression and strike back

118 Roman Krznaric, *The Good Ancestor: How to Think Long Term in a Short-Term World* (London: Penguin, 2021), chap. 6.

119 H.A. Hellyer, "After Afghanistan, let's not be misty-eyed about the West's rules-based order," *Politico*, August 27, 2021, https://www.politico.eu/article/afghanistan-united-states-west -united-kingdom-nato-taliban.

120 For a vision of this future, see Elizabeth C. Economy and Michael Levi, *By All Means Necessary: How China's Resource Quest Is Changing the World* (Oxford: Oxford University Press, 2015); and Elizabeth C. Economy, *The World According to China* (Cambridge: Polity, 2022).

121 Colm Quinn, "Biden Plans Belt and Road Competitor at COP26," *Foreign Policy*, November 2, 2021, https://foreignpolicy.com/2021/11/02/biden-plans-belt-and-road-competitor-at-cop26.

122 Thomas Madden, *Empire of Trust: How Rome Built – and America Is Building – A New World* (New York: Plume, 2009); and Elbridge A. Colby, *The Strategy of Denial: American Defense in an Age of Great Power Conflict* (Princeton: Yale University Press, 2021).

123 Jacqueline L. Hazelton, *Bullets not Ballots: Success in Counterinsurgency Warfare* (Ithaca, N.Y.: Cornell University Press, 2021); and Sumantra Maitra, "The rise and fall of the China Question," *The Critic*, November 1, 2021, https://thecritic.co.uk/the-rise-and-fall-of-the-china -question.

124 Rush Doshi, *The Long Game: China's Grand Strategy to Displace American Order* (Oxford: Oxford University Press, 2021).

125 See generally Alfred Rolington, *Strategic Intelligence for the 21st Century: The Mosaic Method* (Oxford: Oxford University Press, 2013).

where it hurts, not least by inflicting reputational damage and collapsing their high-tech supply chains in stolen technology and semiconductors.[126] The point is for the enemy to be hit with a Wall of Law, the legal equivalent of a Phil Spector composition, whose layers work in seamless concert and cannot be unpicked. Such lawfare is not a panacea, but it is a vital missing tool in the West's armory which, if institutionalized and combined with artful statesmanship, can supplement conventional military force, mitigate domestic vulnerabilities, and take the fight to the enemy.[127] If, in the end, the West emerges victorious over the CCP and law plays a crucial part in that victory, there is every reason to expect the rule of law and rules-based international order to emerge with unrivaled prestige the world over. That, truly, is a prize worth fighting for. So cry 'Havoc,' and let slip the dogs of law!

126 Radomir Tylecote, "Chip Race with China," *The Critic*, November 2, 2021, https://thecritic.co .uk/chip-race-with-china.
127 See Kittrie's 'call to action,' in Kittrie, *Lawfare*, 329–343.

Index

For Product Safety Concerns and Information please contact our EU
representative GPSR@taylorandfrancis.com
Taylor & Francis Verlag GmbH, Kaufingerstraße 24, 80331 München, Germany